Forward From Rebellion
Reconstruction and Revolution In Arkansas
1868-1874

John I. Smith

Rose Publishing Company
Little Rock, Arkansas

Copyright 1983 by John I. Smith

ISBN Number 0-914546-47-3

Library of Congress Card Catalogue Number 83-61504

Except for use in a review, the reproduction or utilization of this work in any form is forbidden without the written permission of the publisher.

Contents

Introduction v

Chapter 1 Punishment Above the Law 1

Chapter 2 Born to Command 21

Chapter 3 The Militia — "Damn You, You Didn't
           Vote Right" 27

Chapter 4 A Waste-Howling Wilderness 41

Chapter 5 An Independent Man Must Be Destroyed 49

Chapter 6 For Once, At Least, Let Us Be One 63

Chapter 7 To Be Governor or Die Trying 75

Chapter 8 The Echo of Powell Clayton 81

Chapter 9 Who Was Elisha Baxter? 87

Chapter 10 A Spirit of Fairness and Earnestness 91

Chapter 11 The Two-Edged Sword of Elisha Baxter 103

Chapter 12 Brooks' Line of March 109

Chapter 13 Coup Against a Good Government 117

Chapter 14 The Father of Arkansas 137

Chapter 15 What Became of the Radicals? 147

Bibliography 159

Authentication

This work avoids quoting popular books written in early impassioned time and relies on few books at all. The libraries have furnished microfilms of the major papers, Journals of General Assemblies and conventions, documents, and other basic material. Other major sources of information were responses to letters written to historical associations, personal visits to many of these organizations, and visits to several state archives. Facts rather than the opinions of other writers have provided the basis of this book.

The index of the *New York Times* gives not only the date but the page and column number of a news item, and that method was adopted in this book with newspaper references — the last two hyphenated figures as in (2-4) meaning page 2, column 4. The *Times* and the *Arkansas Gazette* were the two newspapers most often used, being the most complete, but all extant sources were used.

This book does not document well-known historical items found in all textbooks, and tries not to over-authenticate.

Introduction

The aim in writing this book on Reconstruction has been to find the truth about a tragic era of our history and to narrate that truth into an interesting and unprejudiced story.

This book maintains that neither side of the post-Civil War struggle contained all the angels or all the devils, and, therefore, both compliments and criticisms appear for each side. The book condemns neither Northerners or Southerners, neither whites nor blacks, neither Democrats nor Republicans, but endeavors to tell the truth, as far as it can be determined. It condemns radicals emanating from any group.

Many carpetbaggers, perhaps most of them, were merely immigrants who brought national currency to replace the worthless Confederate money and brought commerce to the stricken South. Many freedmen, especially those with some education or training, stood by the state in its efforts for advancement. No group carries the full blame for the problems of Reconstruction.

The radicals who oppressed Arkansas were often criminals discharged from the Union Army while in the South, migrants from the North, or recruits from the worst element in the old Confederacy. They were aided by the political radicals in Washington, and thus the term "radical" was born there rather than in the South.

While some who came or stayed after being mustered out of the Army did so to help, it must be admitted that those who misbehaved stamped the whole group with an evil reputation. Some essentially good carpetbaggers were led astray by radicals who claimed to be Republicans and demanded that their followers adhere to the principle of "party regularity." Too few of those who wanted only to help found no friendly greetings from the Southern people, and this fact caused the weaker ones to fall in line behind the leading radicals in a course of action that was not the best for the South or the nation.

After all wars, some people behave badly because of atrocities committed during the wars by the opposing side, and they carry the hatreds from the loss of friends or kinsmen. This situation existed after the Civil War, and consequently both sides committed atrocities. There occurred Johnson's Island, Fort Pillow, Andersonville, and the March through Georgia. Two of the above atrocities were charged to each side, and the hatreds caused thereby left a legacy of hatred for decades. Many of the more radical leaders maintained that not to punish the South was to forfeit the victory of Appomattox.

To some people, interest demands not the truth, but a viewpoint that favors the passions of a lifetime. Others look for exciting action and turn away from history to fiction. This book focuses on facts in the hope of discovering how to avoid tragic behavior in the future.

The efforts of the historian should be to erase as many errors as possible and to discover as many heretofore hidden truths as possible. Hundreds of comments, charges, and counter-charges found in this study have failed to meet reasonable standards of human behavior and some first laid-aside charges have been resurrected after further investigations. Many remarks the author heard in the early part of this century from those who lived during the Civil War era have had to be reinterpreted in the light of their aims and the stresses they endured.

Since Reconstruction in all ten states was independent of the others, this book relates what occurred in Arkansas, where the struggle was severe, where militia force gained control of the political destinies of several sections, and where the only open civil war occurred within a state. In many respects the Reconstruction conflict in Arkansas was therefore the most severe of all.

America suffered many losses during the Civil War and Reconstruction which have received proper notice in history. Most lamented was the loss of 600,000 sons. Next in attention was the loss of the servitude of four million slaves, but with that loss we gained four million free people later made citizens, a far more valuable gain. Greatly lamented was the loss of four to six billion dollars in money and property. Next to the loss of life comes the loss of faith which each section had in the other. The extent and causes of this loss of faith have not been so well explained or even understood.

While the hatred on both sides has been intense, this book tries to show that the perpetrators were only a small part of our total population. There were many more good people than bad on each side. Many on both sides were misinformed and their leaders lacked the statesmanship necessary to hold the ship of state on its proper course. Thus radicalism found a fertile field in which to bloom.

All books should show a need for being. Little has been written on Reconstruction in Arkansas in the last sixty years.

The present viewpoints of people should claim a book that thoroughly narrates the larger occurrences and trends and avoids the hundreds of the trivial ones. A good historical narrative should meet racial problems in keeping with twentieth century viewpoints.

A modern version of Reconstruction should give credit to those people in the North who aided the South, to those non-radicals who came to the South and helped her in this struggle, and those blacks who stood for right. Thus this book claims "New Version."

Chapter 1

Punishment Above the Law

Since Arkansas achieved statehood, the most critical decision made by any of the state's elected delegations was the act of secession on May 5, 1861. Arkansas and the other ten states of the Confederacy lost their attempt to form a separate nation at Appomattox on April 9, 1865.

At that point Arkansas was left without a peace treaty from the victorious Union designating what type of government the state would have. Hopes of peaceful government and sovereignty within the old union died the following April 14 with the assassination of Abraham Lincoln. Arkansas was then like a ship without a rudder in a stormy sea.

At the conclusion of the war, Arkansas had two governments: A Unionist government under Isaac Murphy, which Lincoln had helped create in the late winter of 1863-64 and the one faithful to the Confederacy under Harris Flanagin. The Confederate government held the southwest third of the state and on June 15, 1865, surrendered to Murphy, giving all of Arkansas a moderate Unionist government.

Andrew Johnson succeeded Lincoln as president and tried to carry on with Lincoln's amnesty plan, but, although he was advised by a great historian, George Bancroft, Johnson did not possess Lincoln's greatness or diplomacy.

Thus the fight to determine the status of the conquered states began between the radicals in Congress who wanted to punish the South and the conservatives under the President who wanted early readmittance of the seceded states into the Union.

From Isaac Murphy's inauguration as Unionist governor of northern Arkansas on April 18, 1864, until the surrender of General Lee on April 9, 1865, the governor struggled successfully to hold his administration together against poverty, marauders, guerrillas, and other discontents. Then he began his peace-time administration. On May 10, 1865, he issued a peaceful proclamation to the people:

> We have all done wrong. No one can say that his heart is altogether clean, and his hands pure. Then as we wish to be forgiven, let us forgive those who have sinned against us, and ours.
>
> The land is steeped in blood — innocent blood — and defiled with crime. Let us wash it out with tears of sorrow and repentance, works of love, kindness and charity, that peace, good will and confidence may return and swell among us.[1]

The *Arkansas Gazette*, which ceased publication when Little Rock surrendered to the Union forces on September 10, 1863, reappeared on May 10, 1865, and C. C. Danley, the editor, spoke of peace:

> If by our humble aid we assist in bringing order and harmony out of chaos and confusion, in inducing people to cease to hate and learn to 'love one another,' to forget war and learn peace, we shall be more than remunerated.[2]

On May 20 the *Gazette* editor spoke well of Murphy and his message to the people:

> He has done himself and the cause, and the state he represents, honor on this occasion, and the advice which he gives and the encouragement which he lends to all who are not too deaf to hear, and to blind to see, is good throughout.[3]

Murphy, on the recommendation of people in southern Arkansas, appointed to the county positions in his government those men who previously had been elected under the Flanagin government.[4] Thus, a good framework of loyal but not radical government was reconstructed throughout Arkansas. Murphy had successfully brought peace.

The *Gazette* editorial of June 12, 1865, commented that "99 out of 100 of the people of Arkansas support the [Murphy's] Administration." On the following day, the paper stated, " We doubt if there be a state in the Union more entirely supported by its citizens or more worthy of recognition beyond its borders."

On June 15, local citizens held a law and order meeting in Washington, the seat of the Confederate administration. The meeting complimented the Constitution of 1864 and the Murphy Government and advised the people to support the administration. Flanagin returned the Arkansas archives to Little Rock undamaged and ceased his efforts to exercise any authority over the southern part of the state.

Federal General Albert Webb Bishop, who had been appointed adjutant general of Arkansas by Murphy, delivered the Fourth of

July oration at Fayetteville in 1865 and stated: "Those returning inhabitants who have been in rebellion, and now desire to become citizens of the United States Government, should be received fraternally." Perhaps in no other Confederate state was such fraternal behavior engendered.

The July Fourth celebration at Little Rock, though led mostly by pro-Union speakers, refrained from any anti-Southern actions or words. The *Gazette* in its editorial column July 5 spoke in glowing terms of the good will fostered on this occasion:

... and another thing, too, which gave us pleasure to see, was the Old Little Rock Band, that left the city in June '61 with the Capitol Guards. They were paroled with Johnston's Army, and their battered and time worn instruments brought to mind the scenes which they had passed through. They discoursed most excellent music at the head of the Hook and Ladder Company, and it seemed to enjoy hugely of the prospects of again flourishing under the wing of Uncle Samuel.

This moderate Murphy government, established under President Lincoln, needed cooperation from both the Northern radicals and the Southern Confederates. But some Southerners refused to take a moderate position, and the Northern radicals would concede nothing.

The Republican Party in 1860 had won the election against a divided Democratic Party. If the Republicans were to become a majority party they needed to win over those moderate people who had abandoned the Democrats.

Since Congress did not meet as provided by the Constitution until the first Monday in December, 1865, Congressional opposition to the Lincoln-Johnson policy developed rapidly. The delay allowed Wendell Phillips, Thaddeus Stevens, Charles Sumner, and other Congressmen to agitate for punitive measures against the South. Sumner was the leading senator determined to immediately lift the freedmen into full citizenship. Thus, two plans of reconstruction arose — Presidential and Congressional.

The Congress of that date had been elected along with Lincoln in November, 1864, and the radicals elected then did not have sufficient strength to put over punitive measures against the South. They did have sufficient strength to prevent the admittance of either the Unionist government in Arkansas or any kind of self-reconstructed government in the South allowed or promoted by President Johnson. This allowed the sore to fester until after the election in November, 1866, and the delay made agreement less likely.

Considerable opposition then prevailed in the North to punitive measures, and George Bancroft, historian and advisor to President Johnson, on February 16, 1866, the first day that Lincoln's birthday was observed, stated to the joint houses of Congress:

> When I think of the friends I have lost in this war — and everyone who hears me has lost some of those whom he most loved — there is no consolation to be derived from victims on the scaffold or from anything but the established union of the regenerated nation.[5]

After the assassination of Lincoln, no one had a well-defined plan for the seceded states. Lincoln never put his plan on paper, except for his amnesty proclamation, and the punitive spirit in the North grew with every atrocious act or rumor in any insufficiently policed South and with every vindictive speech made by the Northern radicals.

However, the Unionist government of Arkansas had formed a satisfactory administration for both sides. A constitution was adopted March 16, 1864, by a vote of 12,177 to 226;[6] and Isaac Murphy was elected governor with only 25 negative votes. All of this was accomplished with only slight federal assistance.

The 1864 constitution and the Murphy government were not as harsh as the radicals wanted nor as conservative as the ex-Confederates desired. The General Assembly under this constitution in early 1864 ratified the Thirteenth Amendment to the U. S. Constitution abolishing slavery.

Not enough people in the North wanted a liberal policy, and some unwise actions in the South gave ammunition to the radicals. For example, the radicals regarded the black codes, especially the ones passed in Mississippi, as too repressive. In addition, some atrocities occurred in the South, many performed by dangerous men discharged from both armies. They were compounded by the worst of the carpetbaggers, who reported fictitious atrocities. That the atrocities were not as severe as depicted in the North is supported by General Sherman's report on February 2, 1866, to General Ralston, the Chief of Staff in Washington:

> The Negroes in Arkansas can all find profitable and lucrative employment, and are protected in all their rights and property by the civil authorities. I met not one citizen or soldier who questioned or doubted that their freedom was as well assured in Arkansas as in Ohio. Governor Murphy says that the Negroes could obtain title to real estate or any kind of property, and that the courts, both Federal and State, would protect them. . .
> Single individuals now travel unarmed from one part of the state to another; and General Reynolds is rarely called upon to afford military protection to anyone, white or black.[7]

George Bancroft saw the tragic struggle that was developing and tried to bring Sumner and Johnson together in 1865. Both men were too stubborn, however, and the fight continued.

After making a long speech on December 20, 1865, that criticized the South severely, Sumner said of the freedmen:

> In the name of God, let us protect them...An avenging God cannot sleep while such things find countenance. If you are not ready to become the Moses of an oppressed people, do not become its Pharaoh.[8]

Wendell Phillips, probably the most vitriolic speaker in the North, goaded the Republican Party into action and stated on October 17 at Boston in his famous "South Victorious" speech that:

> The Republican Party does not exist; there is a spectre walking over the country in a shroud. But there is no such party. It has not existed since the Baltimore Convention [Republican Nomination Convention of 1864], when it was buried in the will of Abraham Lincoln.[9]

Thaddeus Stevens was even more emotional and on October 3 he spoke at Gettysburg about the President's greeting of Southern visitors: "If the President's language to the Southern delegation be not wrong to the living traitors, it is a mockery to the loyal dead."[10]

These three radicals based their claims primarily upon reports, some true and some false, that the freedmen and Unionists of the South were being persecuted. Due to the lower percentage of freedmen in Arkansas than in other parts of the seceded states, this evil was not as serious in Arkansas as in the deep South.

During this time, the halls of Congress and the public speaker's platforms rang with emotional and hateful oratory which gradually drowned the more moderate voices, and influenced the general election of November, 1866.

On August 6, 1866,[11] Arkansas held her first post-war biennial election for all state and county officers, except governor and secretary of state, whose terms were for four years. The entire Unionist slate elected in 1864 under Lincoln's amnesty plan was swept aside and was replaced by ex-Confederates. Atrocious behavior then began to increase.

Part of the cause of this defeat of the Unionist administration was the adoption of a bill by the General Assembly in 1865 disfranchising those who opposed the state government or served the Confederacy after the Unionist government went into effect April 18, 1864. This angered the returning Confederate soldiers in 1865, even though the Arkansas Supreme Court declared the law *ex post facto* and unconstitutional.

The spirits of the ex-Confederates in 1866 were running high, and Murphy, being a Unionist, suffered from this trend. He was nearly 70 years of age and had suffered many privations. His physique showed it. John S. Dunham, in his paper *Van Buren Press*, then saw fit to use the derogatory term "imbecility," yet mentally he was strong, educated, and courageous, standing by his convictions.

Even though Murphy paid no attention to the remark, a few expanded on it. However, the University of Arkansas historian, D. Y. Thomas, termed him strictly honest and one who provided Arkansas good government in a time it was needed.

The Arkansas General Assembly chosen in the August election went into session November 5, 1866,[12] and immediately rejected the Fourteenth Amendment to the Constitution 24 to 1 in the Senate and 64 to 2 in the House. The radicals demanded this amendment as a condition for readmission to the Union. The Arkansas legislature proposed a resolution commending Jefferson Davis for his good management of the Confederacy and President Johnson for his resistance to Congressional Reconstruction. While this Confederate-minded General Assembly passed no freedmen's code similar to that passed in Mississippi, the legislature made public education, the right to vote and hold office, and jury duty privileges for whites only.

The legislature's school bill made no provision for education of blacks and excluded them from the tax-supported free schools, but did relieve them from paying the two-mill school tax. The General Assembly also passed a labor regulation law which required that labor contracts for longer than a month be in writing and that either party to the contract violating it would owe the other the full amount of money the laborer would have earned had he worked the full time of the contract.[13]

In the meantime, the radicals won the national election of November, 1866, by a substantial majority.[14] The unreconstructed South sent senators and representatives to Congress who were not accepted, thus reducing possible conservative strength.

The rejection of the Fourteenth Amendment and other pro-Confederate behavior were perhaps serious mistakes for Arkansas. The Confederate General Assembly in December, 1866, at a cost of $8,016 sent a delegation headed by the respected Reverend Andrew Hunter to Washington to lobby for the Murphy government as organized under the Constitution of 1864.[15]

The group talked to President Johnson, Secretary of State William H. Seward, Attorney General Henry Stanbery, Secretary of War Edwin M. Stanton, General Ulysses S. Grant, and others.[16] At that time, these officials, mostly conservatives, were trying to get another state in addition to Tennessee of the eleven seceded states to ratify the Fourteenth Amendment and hoped that if Arkansas would ratify, others would follow.

The Arkansas delegation asked Grant if Arkansas would be readmitted into the Union if she ratified the Fourteenth Amendment. The general assured them that he could see no reason why not. Considering Grant's power and the near certainty he would be the next President, agreeing to his wishes would have been a logical move for the Arkansas delegation to make. The decision might have influenced others to follow, and the radicals in Congress would have been stymied in their efforts to pass Reconstruction bills that aimed to force the adoption of the Fourteenth and Fifteenth Amendments.

The committee came back to Arkansas believing that Congress would never destroy a state, and the General Assembly never considered ratifying the amendments. Arkansas thus lost her only hope of continuing under a moderate constitution.

This all happened during the third year of Governor Isaac Murphy's term. In his message to the 1866-67 General Assembly (known as the Confederate legislature) he warned the members to take a compromising attitude:

> This is the Congressional scheme of Reconstruction, and has been made the leading issue in the late election, and sustained by large majorities.
> Though not all the insurgent states could desire, it becomes a very grave question for the legislature to decide whether any terms more favorable are likely to be obtained by opposition, or whether it is not the better policy for the state to accept the proposed terms, and then secure the prompt reconstruction of the state into harmonious action with the governing states, and on an equality with them in the Union.
> Judging from the results of the late elections and from the decided tone of public sentiment in the states that subdued the insurrection, it is not probable that better terms will be granted. The effect of rejection on the prosperity and happiness of the people of the state, demands solemn consideration.

The Southern press paid little attention to Murphy's advice. However, the *New York Times* of November 23 printed Governor Murphy's message in full and stated:

> But Governor Murphy earns credit for sagacity and moral courage when he undertakes to recommend the ratification of the Amendment on the grounds of expediency. He does not say that the terms please him, but he correctly interprets the recent election as a sign that no better terms will be offered. His method of stating the case is mild, but unanswerable . . . Governor Murphy's method of stating the case is equivalent to

an answer ... How far the moderation and prudence of Governor Murphy are shared by the Legislature of Arkansas remains to be seen.

Before the newly-elected Congress took office on March 4, 1867, the old one saw how the Northern people were leaning and passed the first reconstruction bill, the Military District Bill, over President Johnson's veto on March 2, 1867.[17] The retiring Congress, which had had a series of disagreements with Johnson, provided that the newly-elected assembly should meet immediately rather than in December as provided in the Constitution. The new Congress, with more radicals than the previous one, on March 23 (also over Johnson's veto) passed a supplement to the first Reconstruction Act.

These two acts divided the South into five districts,[18] each directed by a federal army official at or above the rank of brigadier general who would be appointed by the President. While the act did not invalidate the Southern state governments, the directors were given all power, even to remove any officer, including the governor. The actions of Congress disfranchised the ex-Confederates and extended the right to vote to the freedmen. The states were required to hold constitutional conventions and to vote on the resulting constitutions. They also were required to adopt the Fourteenth Amendment to the Constitution. Each director had the responsibility of ensuring that these provisions were carried out. After all this was accomplished, any formerly seceded state could apply to Congress for readmittance into the Union.

The radical carpetbaggers, supported by Congress, saw an opportunity to dominate Southern politics. Their strength would be primarily in the newly franchised blacks, the disfranchisement of the ex-Confederates, the use of federal troops if needed, and the orders of Congress delivered to the directors. Thereafter the radicals planned to tie themselves to the Republican Party and make the party supreme in the South. Thus, the new government would be congressional and radical, not Presidential and conservative.

In order to police and rebuild the broken South and for both sides to make friends and learn that each other had merit, military occupation was needed at least for a year or two after Appomattox. The good treatment of Lee's Army by Grant would have been a good beginning. To wait two years for such actions was disastrous.

In the summer of 1866 the impoverished South was visited by a calamitous drouth which brought starvation to her poor people in the following winter of 1866-1867. While this military district or Reconstruction bill was being debated, Congress passed a sizeable relief appropriation bill. The Southern Farmers Relief Association which was centered in New York (Congressional Record, Volume 38, pp. 72-74) relates how these two aids, though opposed by some, substantially aided hundreds of thousands of starving people. Letters from Federal General O.O. Howards and from poet John Greenleaf Whittier asking for aid were read. This relief shows that when properly informed, Congress took better stands. There was trouble in Arkansas and in the South, and there were many untruthful charges which confused some of them.

Some of the trouble was caused by the turmoil and social change that follows any war and by the radicals in driving a wedge between the races.

Many Northern people wanted to receive the South on a fraternal basis in the beginning days of peace, while others did not. The latter group grew in subsequent years, and those who wanted to punish the South took a large part in implementing the new order.

General Edward O.C. Ord was made Director of District Four,[19] Mississippi and Arkansas, and on April 5, 1868, he appointed General C.H. Smith his assistant in Arkansas. Ord and Smith were strict but fair men who enforced all laws, including the Reconstructions Acts, without hatred. General Smith had earlier rendered meritorious service in the Freedman's Bureau. Three days after Ord appointed him as assistant, Smith issued his circular No. 2, which advised the freedmen:

> Freedmen are cautioned against undue excitement growing out of local political conventions ... They must realize that the highest privileges of freedmen do not absolve them from labor; that even the right and privilege of voting will not provide them with food, raiment, and shelter ... In consequence of the backwardness of the season, every day's labor in the field at this time is of utmost importance, and the plow must not halt in the furrow if the laborer expects to make a crop.[20]

On assuming command, Ord issued a liberal order on March 26 asking existing officials to enforce the law:

> ... so as to obviate as far as possible the necessity to the exercize of military authority under the law of Congress passed March 2, 1867, creating the military districts.[21]

One of Ord's first administrative acts was to order $200,000 in state funds to be invested in government bonds. Treasurer Henry Page asked that the order be cut to $100,000 and Ord granted that request. L.B. Cunningham had been elected treasurer, but Ord replaced him with Page because his confederate career made him untenable. Governor Murphy, on Ord's order, notified all county officials to account to Ord all monies collected and paid out[22] and notified the General Assembly that it could not meet again.

One incident illustrates how Ord could be just, if allowed to be. In August, 1867, the *Constitutional Eagle*, a newspaper, complained of the behavior of some drunken Federal soldiers. The soldiers, led by Major George S. Pierce, on August 8[23] retaliated by looting the newspaper building and throwing the type and equipment into the Ouachita River. Colonel C.C. Gilbert, the post commander, wrote to Ord on August 15 in answer to his request for information: "... the military forces detailed to enable him [General Ord] to perform his duties, are not the servants of the people of Arkansas, but rather their master."[24] Ord replied:

> Your assertion that the military forces are not the servants of the people of Arkansas, but rather their masters, is unjust, both to the people and military and unfounded in fact. The Military forces are servants of the law, and the laws are for the benefit of the people . . . Your assumption that a party of soldiers could, at their own option, forceably destory a citizen's property and commit gross violations of public peace would not be tolerated under a 'Napoleon.'[25]

At the trial a short time later General Ord stated, "Major Pierce seems not to have been aware that untruthful criticism does not provoke a man of sense, but that newspaper comments are resented only in proportion to their fidelity of fact."

Subsequently Major Pierce, Commander of the 28th Infantry which gutted the newspaper office, was courtmartialed, reprimanded, fined a year's pay, and reduced in rank. The military apparently respected the freedom of the press, and the Arkansas press went on a rampage of speaking its mind. The *Arkansas Gazette* suggested that the punishment was too light, and that the officer should have been completely expelled from the Army and sent to the penitentiary.[26] In January 1868, the *Constitutional Eagle*, with fresh capital, began publishing anew with an appropriate motto: "The military forces are the servants of the laws, and the laws are for the benefit of the people."

The radicals in all these activities wished to make themselves synonomous with the Republican Party. Many radical papers sprang up over the state, and the principal one became the *Republican* of Little Rock. Sometimes the paper was called the *Evening Republican*, sometimes the *Morning Republican*. The *Republican* began in 1867 and served primarily as a propoganda sheet. Its viewpoint was strictly opposed to all Southern traditions. Soon after it began the paper stated: "The rights of those who engaged in the rebellion are just such, and no other, as the conquering powers see fit to accord."[27]

The people approved much of what the military did while maintaining a dislike of the radicals. The *Arkansas Gazette* felt that Ord was trying to do a good job: "If the Commanding General does not shape his course after the dictates of the elect, and look more carefully after the interests of the annointed." The paper warned, "He need not be surprised to be metamorphosed into a rebel sympathizer or a disloyal copperhead."[28]

The *Gazette* proved to be prophetic, and Ord was removed in December, 1867 because of the clamor of the radicals. The director was succeeded by General Alvan C. Gillem.

The diary of Gideon Welles, Secretary of the Navy in the Lincoln-Johnson administration, indicates that, according to General Grant, Ord was a very honest and careful man and had wanted to resign for several months; and that Gillem was in line for either Pope's or Ord's place. The high point of the work of these two directors was that the registration of those able to vote under the terms of the Reconstruction Acts was completed in September, 1867.

The registration was a one-sided affair, if the registrars so decided. Not only did they exclude ex-Confederates from registering to vote but also excluded their relatives, supporters, or those who opposed Congressional reconstruction. The last Reconstruction Act had been passed July 19, 1867, and it allowed the registrars to scratch off anyone they wished and write in any freedman's name who had not registered. The real campaign over the calling of a constitutional convention then began.

Some conservative speakers told the freedmen to vote with them because they had lived here and knew what was best. On the other hand, the radical speakers answered that they were the ones who fought for freedom for the slaves while their opponents had fought for continued enslavement. The latter argument won the support of the freedmen.[29] The election on a constitutional convention and for delegates to the convention was held November 5, and the voters approved the convention 27,576 to 13,588. Following poor advice, many whites refused to vote.[30]

The constitutional convention convened in Little Rock January 8, 1868, and the radicals outnumbered the conservatives about 44 to 7, with about 17 undecided. Twenty-three of the delegates were strangers to Arkansas, and their leaders were Joseph Brooks, a Methodist minister from Iowa; James C. Hinds from New York; and Thomas M. Bowen from Kansas. Eight delegates were black, and one, W.H. Grey from Phillips County and Virginia, had some political education. Grey, Brooks, and Hinds spoke from one to two hours at a time and Brooks, the most vocal, was called "Mr. Convention."

Bowen was a young and careless, although capable, individual. Early in the war he enlisted in the 13th Regiment of Kansas, which served entirely in the Missouri, Arkansas, Kansas, and Oklahoma sector of limited activities. He received a number of promotions, finally to Brevet Brigadier General in the last months of the war.

On June 28, 1865, he was dishonorably dismissed,

... for attempting to defraud justice, by sending to the War Department a false statement, with a view of setting aside an order of dismissal in the case of Capt. James H. McDougal, 13th Kansas Volunteers, and enclosing in said statement a receipt for certain moneys belonging to enlisted men in said McDougal's company, knowing the same to have been antedated, in order to cover up the guilt of the said McDougal.[31]

Just how close Bowen was to the fraud or how he participated is not clear from the General Service Administration report. However, the order of June 28 was revoked December 5, 1865, upon satisfactory payment of all money due the government. This affair could have been a factor in Bowen's failure to return to his Kansas home in 1865.

Jesse N. Cypert from White County, a Unionist before the war, represented the conservative minority. He was a frail, quiet, logical man whose following during the convention rose from 7 delegates to about 20.

The convention elected Bowen president and he held the meetings in as proper order as any man could. The convention employed more doorkeepers and sergeants at arms than needed and furnished each member with ten daily papers. On the third day, Cypert tried to prevent this expense by reducing the number of papers to three per day, but failed by a vote of 14 to 45. Cypert, on the sixth day, also moved that the delegates simply adopt the Constitution of 1864 (Unionist Constitution) and go home, and Hinds retaliated by a motion that the matter be referred to the Committee on the Penitentiary. Pandemonium then set in and never abated.

On January 16, the *Gazette* spoke of the convention in acid terms:
When we designated in Tuesday's issue, the piebald convention as a 'bastard collection whose putridity stinks in the nostrils of all decency,' we made use of no terms which can properly be designated as Billingsgate. These words express no undeserved abuse. They are descriptive of the character of the assemblage. That the body is illegal, illegitimate and therefore a political bastard is beyond all question...

Fraud has been the distinguished feature of every step taken to dry nurse the bastard into vigorous existence.

This type of condemnation represented the spirit of the era. The radicals had the majority to run the convention as they pleased and only allowed the conservatives one man on almost every committee. One furor was caused by John M. Bradley, a radical minister from Bradley County, who introduced a resolution in the 18th day (January 29) against miscegenation. This resolution created a heated debate. The measure did not pass, but Bradley abandoned the radical group. He voted against the whole constitution with these words:

> I ask to bequeath to my posterity no greater boon, than to record my vote against that damnable engine of oppression and ruin. I ask that my language be cut in rock and lead be poured into letters, to stand forever. I vote 'Nay.'[32]

The Constitution was finished on February 10 or in the early morning of the 11th. Cypert and 20 followers voted "no," and 16 refused to sign the document. It was not a bad constitution except that it gave the chief executive entirely too much appointive power and had too few restraints upon him and the General Assembly. This later enabled the radicals to run wild. The constitution also ended the terms of all state, district, and county officials and provided for a new election. This suited the radicals because they intended to capture all offices and dominate the state.

Article 1 of the schedule of the constitution set the election for the approval or disapproval of the constitution and the election of the few state and county officials not appointed by the governor plus representatives in Congress for March 13. The election could run as long as the election commission determined. The radicals held their nominating convention for state officers January 15, while the Constitutional Convention remained in session.[33] Powell Clayton, who was not a delegate to the Constitutional Convention, spent his time gathering support in the radical party. He received the nomination for governor over the Arkansas Unionist James M. Johnson by a vote of 112 to 49. The Unionists were disappointed that the carpetbaggers had seized leadership from them so soon, but Johnson was unanimously nominated for lieutenant governor. Robert T.J. White was nominated for Secretary of State; James R. Berry for Auditor; and Lafayette Gregg, Thomas M. Bowen, and John McClure for the Supreme Court.[34] McClure was a carpetbagger and a close ally of Clayton.

The conservatives held their convention January 27[35] and decided to put no candidates in the field but rather hoped to challenge the entire procedure in federal court. Their whole platform could be summed up in the following slogans: "A white man's government in a white man's country" and "Equality of the Negro before the law, but not his power over the law."

The three men on the election commission established by Section 4 of the schedule of the constitution were Thomas M. Bowen, Joseph Brooks, and James Hodges — all carpetbaggers. The election that began March 13 was scheduled to end March 27. The conservatives massed a campaign of intimidation against potential black voters, while the radicals marched freedmen from poll to poll. In Pulaski County 1,195 more votes were cast than the number registered, and the radicals carried the county by 3,922.[36]

General Gillem, Ord's replacement, received the results in Vicksburg, and announced that the constitution had carried 27,913 to 26,597. From that date until July 2, 1867, the radicals controlled only the General Assembly, and General Gillem, through Governor Murphy, controlled the executive branch of the government.

According to the new constitution, the newly elected General Assembly was required to convene on April 2, about five days after the election ended. The rumor persisted that Gillem would recognize the General Assembly and not bother the members unless they tried to seize the treasury or remove state officers.[37] The radical legislators, Murphy, and the other Unionist officers were subject to the director until Arkansas was readmitted into the Union.

The radicals seemed to feel that their complete domination of Arkansas was assured. The *Republican* stated:

> ... they [conservatives] will be at a disadvantage as hereafter those voting 'no' will be disfranchised ... They have run their last race in Arkansas. After this comes the judgment.[38]

After the war many bitter-end secessionists fled to the west or to Latin America, but the radicals avoided the Unionists as well as the secessionists and denied both groups any strong place in the new government. On the other hand, the conservatives, not being dominated by the avowed secessionists, developed leadership rapidly. A few blacks also proved that they could decide issues on principle, not radical pressure. The two black ministers, brothers, J.T. White of Helena and R.B. White of Pulaski, Dr. A.M. Johnson of Mississippi County, and W.H. Furbush of Phillips County were blacks who refused to buckle under radical pressure. Blackwell Shelton, a black minister of Monticello, said:

> I will cast my lot with them [the white] in the reorganization of the country, believing that our interests are one and the same with theirs, and whatever influence I may have shall be exerted in cementing the bonds of union between the white and the black man, that peace, harmony, and prosperity may prevail.[39]

The other state and county officers elected under the new

constitution could take office as soon as they received their certificates of election from the election commission, but they would have had questionable status until Gillem declared the passage of the constitution. Isaac Murphy, a Unionist, continued to administer the government, subject to General Gillem's direction.

Even though General Gillem did not declare the constitution adopted until April 23, the General Assembly was notified to meet by the election commission and promptly met in Little Rock on April 2.[40] The House elected John G. Price, a carpetbagger, as speaker.[41] James M. Johnson, who was elected lieutenant governor the previous week, was ex-officio President of the Senate. The General Assembly promptly adopted the Fourteenth Amendment to the U. S. Constitution, elected radicals Alexander McDonald and B.F. Rice as United States Senators, passed a resolution supporting the impeachment of President Johnson, and asked Congress to readmit Arkansas into the Union.[42]

Although the newly elected Senator McDonald was listed as a radical, he did have many desirable characteristics. The conservative *Gazette* of May 8, 1866, recounted how McDonald came to the Fort Smith area in the latter days of the war with a train of eighty wagons containing provisions for the people. Most of the wagons were captured by bushwhackers, but some reached their destination. He later established a bank and a merchandising firm in Fort Smith, and a bank in Little Rock by 1866.[43] These activities brought both needed goods and a stable currency to Arkansas.

B.F. Rice had been a member of the state House of Representatives of Kentucky.[44] Before election to the U.S. Senate, reports surfaced that he came to the Union army during the war from Winchester, Kentucky, after collecting $4,000 for a man's estate and then keeping the money for himself. The legislature elected him to the Senate by a big majority.[45] While this charge is hard to prove or disprove today, it was consistently charged at the time, even by Clayton after the two had a falling out.[46]

The two elections which provided for a convention and later adopted the Constitution of 1868 were the first ones in which the ex-Confederates were disfranchised and the blacks granted the right to vote.

The *New York Times*, a Republican paper, commented:
We concede that the action of Congress has been unwise. Very much of it has been, in our judgment, unsuited to the necessities of the case, not at all calculated to heal the wounds of war, or serve wisely the problems which the war created.[47]

While Joseph Brooks had been a power in the Constitutional Convention and was chairman of the Republican Nominating

Convention, he was watched closely by the Powell Clayton faction of the radical party. Brooks was a candidate for both U. S. Senate seats and received a token vote in each race (about a fourth of the whole) but was easily defeated by the two relatively unknown party faithfuls.[48] This showed that Clayton had the power to select two Senators. While Brooks had played a major role in the Constitutional Convention, Clayton had been quietly building his power with the radical wing of the machine.

The new assembly continued the radical policy of squandering funds. For example, when John N. Tobias, a representative from Phillips County, died on April 10, the legislature found the money to send the body and the family to their real home in Washington County, Illinois. The assembly also paid the burial expenses and considered paying the family of Tobias the per diem and mileage that he would have received and in fact did so after Powell Clayton became governor.[49] It also sent a delegation from each house to accompany the remains.

Just as the Constitutional Convention had done, this General Assembly provided each member with ten dailies of his choice, or their equal in weeklies, to subsidize the radical papers that had little other paid circulation. It also elected an excessive number of clerks, sergeants-at-arms, wood choppers, and doorkeepers, which gave their black followers needed jobs.

Nothing of importance was left for the 1868 General Assembly to do until Governor-elect Powell Clayton took office. Valentine Dell, an editor, educator, and senator from Fort Smith, introduced a measure April 20 to adjourn until reconvened by proper authorities and said, "This was the first General Assembly under a republican form of government and ought to set a high example of integrity . . . We are in a state of suspense injurious to us . . . that an expense of $25,000 would be saved the impoverished people."[50] Dell's was the only voice in the General Assembly that opposed the radical regime.[51] He was a German who immigrated after the revolution of 1848. However, other honorable men gradually emerged to give the radicals respectable opposition. Dell's resolution was buried in the Ways and Means Committee. Members were often absent, but a bill to deny them pay was defeated. Though a Republican, Dell was utterly independent, commending or criticizing either Republican or Democratic moves, depending on their effect.[52]

Customarily, officers serve until their successors are elected and qualified. Powell Clayton, who ran unopposed in the election of late March 1868, perhaps could have qualified and occupied the gubernatorial office at any time, but he still would have been under Generals Gillem and Smith. Since Clayton wanted full control, he waited until Arkansas was readmitted into the Union and the generals were removed.

The General Assembly, from the time of Dell's efforts at adjournment until July 2 (over two months) did practically nothing. They met, discussed a few inconsequential questions, and adjourned until the next day when they would repeat the procedure. The journals of that session show such motions as to change the court dates in certain counties from April and October to May and November. The assembly considered requests for leaves of absence and bills for the members' own compensation. They depicted the Republican Party as synonymous with loyalty, honor, and progress, and the Democratic party with disloyalty, dishonor, and rebellion. They submitted no bills to Governor Murphy for his consideration, but did bring bills through the second reading, waiting to pass and submit them to Governor Clayton after his inauguration.

Samuel Bard, representative from Washington County, announced that he would introduce a measure to make the inmates of the penitentiary wear Confederate military uniforms, with murderers entitled to wear the uniform of a colonel and other uniforms distributed according to the extent of the prisoner's crime. Bard's remark was typical of many radical legislators.

Even though during the first two years after the war the carpetbaggers lived in the South fairly anonymously, deed records show they were acquiring good real estate through tax forfeitures and foreclosure and estate sales. Some carpetbaggers went into merchandising. As merchants, they performed perhaps the greatest aid to the people of the South by bringing in U.S. currency to replace the worthless Confederate currency. Many Northerners came to help the war-torn South and did a lot of good in spite of some opposition. For example, the great minister-teacher, Enoch K. Miller, established a number of schools for freedmen in Arkansas. This illustrious London-born Union soldier was shot through the body in the last minutes of the Battle of Gettysburg but survived to do excellent work in Arkansas.[53] Many others like Miller expressed no enmity toward the South and did only honorable service. Soon after Appomattox, the daughter of John Brown began teaching black children in Richmond in the abandoned home of former Governor Wise of Virginia. Ironically, Wise had been governor when John Brown was executed for taking the arsenal at Harper's Ferry in 1859, and had refused clemency for Brown.[54]

The daughter of the deceased Congressman Owen Lovejoy was found teaching black children in Vicksburg, Mississippi. Owen Lovejoy was the brother of the martyred Elijah Parrish Lovejoy, killed while defending his printing press from a pro-slavery mob.[55]

Nor should we forget Mattie Stevenson, for she came to Memphis from Illinois during the yellow fever epidemic of September-October, 1873, when as many as 50 per day were dying in Memphis alone. She waited on the sick day and night until she died of the disease.[56] The next year Memphis built a monument in her honor.

On June 22, Arkansas was readmitted into the Union by the Senate over President Johnson's veto by a vote of 30 to 7.[57] The newly elected Congressmen from Arkansas, James Hinds, Logan H. Roots, and Thomas Boles, and Senators Alexander McDonald and Benjamin Rice, were then admitted to their respective houses. Powell Clayton set the date of his inauguration for July 2, giving him time to work up an impressive affair. A new day for Arkansas was about to begin, but soon became the greatest debauchery in the state's history.

FOOTNOTES

[1] *Arkansas Gazette*, May 15, 1865, 2-2. Family records and Isaac Murphy file, Arkansas History Commission, Little Rock.

[2] *Ibid.*

[3] Family records of Isaac Murphy file, Arkansas History Commission, Little Rock.

[4] B.F. Teft, *Speeches of Daniel Webster*, (New York: Lincoln Century Association), p. 561.

[5] Congressional *Globe*, 39th Congress, first session, Vol. 36, p. 504.

[6] Dallas T. Herndon, *Highlights of Arkansas History*, (Little Rock: Arkansas History Commission, 1922), p. 104. Hereafter just Herndon.

[7] *Arkansas Gazette*, February 12, 1866, 1-2.

[8] Congressional *Globe*, 39th Congress, Vol. 36, First Session, p. 95.

[9] *Arkansas Gazette*, November 4, 1865, 1-2.

[10] *Ibid.*, November 4, 1865, 1-8.

[11] *Arkansas Gazette*, August 7, 1866, 2-1.

[12] *Ibid.*, November 6, 1866, 2-2, and November 12, 1866, 2-1.

[13] *Acts of General Assembly of Arkansas, 1866-67*, Act 28, p. 84, approved January 31, 1867.

[14] John Spencer Bassett, *A Short History of the United States*, (New York: McMillan), p. 607. Hereafter just Bassett.

[15] *Journal of the General Assembly of 1866*, p. 67.

[16] New York *Herald*, January 6, 1867, 8-1.

[17] Bassett, *A Short History of the United States*, p. 609.

[18] *Ibid.*

[19] Herndon, p. 109.

[20] *New York Times*, April 21, 1867, 3-6; *Arkansas Gazette*, April 8, 1867.

[21] *Arkansas Gazette*, April 3, 1867.

[22] *Ibid.*, April 28, 1867, 4-1 and 2-5.

[23] *Ibid.*, October 23, 1867.

[24] *New York Times*, September 16, 1867, 1-3.

[25] *Arkansas Gazette*, August 13, 1867, 2-2.

[26] *Ibid.*, October 23, 1867, 1-1 and 2-1.

[27] *The Republican*, July 11, 1867, 2-1. Several small circulation papers of Arkansas used the term "Republican" but here it refers only to the Little Rock *Republican*.
[28] *Arkansas Gazette*, June 12, 1867, 1-2.
[29] *Ibid.*, November 1, 1867, 2-4.
[30] *Ibid.*, November 25, 1867, 2-1.
[31] General Service Administration report on Bowen's military activities from beginning to dismissal.
[32] Journal of Arkansas Constitutional Convention of 1868, third day, p. 59.
[33] *Arkansas Gazette*, January 16, 1868, 2-2.
[34] *Republican*, January 16, 1868, 2-1.
[35] *Arkansas Gazette*, January 28, 1868, 2-2.
[36] *Ibid.*, November 3, 1867, 2-1; and *New York Times*, April 2, 1868, 4-2.
[37] *Republican*, March 27, 1868, 2-1.
[38] *Republican*, March 27, 1868, 2-1.
[39] Weekly *Gazette*, May 28, 1867, 2-3.
[40] *Arkansas Gazette*, April 3, 1868, 2-1.
[41] *Ibid.*, April 4, 1868, 2-1, and *New York Times*, April 5, 1868, 8-1.
[42] *Ibid.*, April 9, 1868, 3-2, and *New York Times*, April 2, 1868, 4-2.
[43] Van Buren *Press*, September 28, 1866, 2-3.
[44] *Arkansas Gazette*, April 14, 1868, 2-1, and *New York Times*, April 2, 1868, 4-2.
[45] *Ibid.*, April 14, 1868, 2-1 of *Arkansas Gazette*.
[46] John M. Harrell, Brooks and Baxter War, p. 137.
[47] *New York Times*, May 9, 1869, 1-6 and 1-8, and May 11, 1-4.
[48] *Arkansas Gazette*, April 15, 1868, 2-1.
[49] *Republican*, April 16, 1868, 2-3. Also *Acts of Arkansas*, 1868, Act 13, p. 37.
[50] *Acts of Arkansas*, 1868, p. 37, and *Republican*, April 21, 1868, 2-2.
[51] Fred Allsopp, *History of the Arkansas Press*, p. 418.
[52] *Republican*, May 16, 1868, 2-2.
[53] Larry Leslie Pierce, "Enoch K. Miller and the Freedmen's Schools," *Arkansas Historical Quarterly*, Vol. XXXI, (1972, No. 4) pp. 305-328.
[54] Fort Smith *New Era*, May 27, 1865, 1-3.
[55] Van Buren *Press*, April 28, 1866, 1-5.
[56] Memphis *Daily Appeal*, October 10, 1873, 1-2.
[57] *Republican*, June 24, 1868, 2-2.

Chapter 2

Born to Command

Powell Clayton was inaugurated governor July 2, 1868. His followers were several hundred men who came from the North after the war or failed to return home after being discharged from the Union Army. His followers also included most of the original Arkansas Unionists, most of the enfranchised blacks, and a few ex-Confederates (Scalawags). These groups constituted the radical party. Their only official acts before July 2, 1868, were in controlling the elections of 1867, formulating the Constitution of 1868, and controlling the acts of the General Assembly which met on April 2, 1868.

Southerners were far more numerous than Clayton's supporters and had aligned with a few northerners, blacks and Arkansas Unionists, but these conservatives were largely disfranchised.

The officials elected in March, 1868, could have taken office as soon as they were notified by the election commission, and they were required to do so within 15 days of notification,[1] but they were not to have full powers until Congress readmitted Arkansas into the Union. Thus, governor-elect Clayton waited until after Arkansas was readmitted. This occurred June 22, 1868, and Clayton set the date of his inauguration for the following July 2. Some county officials had taken office before this date, but many of them waited for Clayton to set the pace and format of their behavior.

Powell Clayton was born in Chester, Pennsylvania, August 7, 1833. Nearby in Delaware was another family of Claytons, of whom John Middleton Clayton, U.S. Senator and later Secretary of State under Presidents Zachary Taylor and Millard Fillmore, was the best known. He negotiated the Clayton-Bulwar treaty of 1850 between the United States and England dealing with the Isthmus of Panama (and a possible canal). The two families of Claytons were cousins, about three generations separated, and had a long history of prominent positions in England dating back to William the Conqueror.[2] Powell Clayton had two younger twin brothers with him in Arkansas named John Middleton and William Henry Harrison Clayton, both of whom played an important role in the radical struggles. Both families of Claytons were strong in their Whig beliefs, as shown by the prominent Whig names of Clayton's younger brothers.

Educated at the military academy at Bristol, Pennsylvania, Powell Clayton went to Atchison, Kansas, as an engineer around 1855. There he became a Democrat. He joined the Union Army in 1861 and came into Arkansas with General Steel in 1863, where he gained a reputation in the defense of federally occupied Pine Bluff against an attack by Confederate General John S. Marmaduke on October 25, 1863.

After the war, Clayton purchased a large plantation near Pine Bluff, married Ben Adaline McGraw of Helena December 14, 1856,[3] and began taking a leading part in radical politics. The McGraws were hotel keepers in Helena catering to the Mississippi steamboat trade and, like most of the business people of that river port, were probably Northern Whigs before the war.

John M. Harrell's book, *The Brooks-Baxter War*, states that Clayton first offered his services in politics to the Southern Democrats. Clayton suggested that he become the party's Representative in Congress, but the Democrats in Pine Bluff refused to accept his offer. However, many Southerners admired Clayton, and some people remarked that by the time he became governor, that Powell Clayton was "born to command."

In Powell Clayton's memoirs published August, 1914, just before his death, he spoke of his inauguration:

About 10 a.m. along the mainstreet leading to the Capitol an open carriage with a military escort approached. The back seat was occupied by two men, the one on the right being about sixty-five years old; the other, about thirty-five. The elder, clad in the homespun garb of a mountaineer, noted the more fashionable attire of the younger man and said: 'Why do you wear gloves in July? Only dudes wear gloves in summertime.' The younger man took no offense, but quickly replied: 'Governor, in deference to your opinion, and especially in view of the character of the work I am about to enter upon today, which will doubtless require "handling without gloves," I will remove mine.' Both men cordially grasped hands, the older remarking: 'I appreciate the magnitude of the work you are about to undertake. May God help you.'

Upon entering the executive office I saw before me, placed upon the opposite wall, a long table with three convenient drawers and on the table a case of open pigeon holes. There was no carpet on the floor, and the rest of the furniture consisted of about two dozen homemade split-bottom chairs.[4]

Clayton was comparing Isaac Murphy (who was nearly 69 years old, not 65) with himself; and the words "homespun garb," "no carpets on the floor," and "split-bottom chairs," were used in derision. Keenly aware of Arkansas' poverty-stricken condition, Murphy spent no money on frills.

Clayton was an accomplished speaker and, as expected, he condemned those who opposed Congressional Reconstruction or opposed the "new class of voters" (freedmen). He showed contempt for the Murphy government by telling the General Assembly that they were the first to assemble in seven years, and he indicated that he would use the militia, if necessary, to enforce the laws. "Idle hours," he stated, "are spent in invectives against the new voters... A bright day is dawning in Arkansas."[5]

"We hope so, most devoutly," replied the *Gazette*.

After Clayton's inauguration, he proceeded to draw pay for the three previous months less one day; that is, for the time he was first eligible to take office. He took $1,236.10 in salary and $300 for house rent.[6] John McClure, in this 1868 election named Associate Justice, received this same salary raise, and also drew pay for some time he did not serve.[7] While the behavior of the radicals in the previous elections and in the convention had been questionable, the Arkansas people believed that Clayton would make a good governor. But taking the unearned money dimmed that hope. The compliant legislature had authorized these extra salaries.

During the Clayton administration, the General Assembly passed an act providing that counties, by popular vote, could provide railroad construction aid up to $100,000 per county and passed another act providing for state bonds for railroads up to $11,400,000.[8] Under this latter act, the state would issue its bonds to railroads already supported by federal land grants up to $10,000 per mile, and to railroads not supported by federal land grants up to $15,000 per mile. The railroads applying for these bonds could sell them for whatever they could get and were to repay them according to their terms. Since they were state obligation bonds, the state could take over the railroads if they failed to pay the bonds. The railroads could apply for the bonds whenever given mileages were completed. A specified mileage and amount per mile for each railroad was stated in the Act.[9]

In addition to specific amounts provided for a number of railroads, the Cairo and Fulton Railroad was offered $3,000,000 in bonds. This was the best organized and best financed railroad in Arkansas, and its officials promptly refused this offer. The Cairo and Fulton intended to pay all its debts, not to avoid them through bankruptcy, which many railroads subsequently did.[10] The term was 30 years and the interest rate 7 per cent, but there was no regulation as to how the bonds were to be sold, no requirement that they sell at any percent of par, or how the money was to be spent.

This railroad aid act had to be approved in the general election of 1868. The railroads were to constitute the arteries of commerce and pattern of progress of the future, and the people wanted railroads, and they willingly voted for the act by 23,984 to 5,210,[11] even though the ballot read only "for railroads," and "against railroads." However, as time passed, the administration of this act was one of several sources of dishonesty and a final cause of the downfall of the radical regime. The poorly managed railroads took the bonds as if they would never have to repay them. Prominent radicals became leading officers and board members of these railroads and sold the bonds or handed them out freely in return for favors.

After spending the $220,000 which former Governor Murphy had left in the treasury, the General Assembly adjourned on July 23 and provided that it should meet again on the third Tuesday in November. This was a crucial date since it followed the Presidential election of November 3, 1868. Clayton, always a shrewd politician, knew that Horatio Seymour and Francis P. Blair, Democratic nominees for president and vice-president, had little chance to defeat U.S. Grant and Schuyler Colfax, the Republican nominees.

One of the first breaks from the radical force occurred July 20 when General John Edwards of Fort Smith wrote ex-Confederate General James F. Fagan that while he had previously been a Republican, he could no longer remain in that party:

If we expect peace, and future prosperity and happiness for the whole country, we must have a radical change, and redeem the country from radical misrule, despotism, and corruption.

General Edwards's opinion was formed not so much by what Powell Clayton had done in twenty days, but by what the radicals had done in the past fifteen months.

The General Assembly just adjourned included such well-known radicals as D.P. Upham, R.F. Catterson, M.L. Stephenson, E.D. Rushing, J.W. Mason, S.W. Mallory, O.P. Snyder, D.P. Beldin, O.A. Hadley, J.N. Sarber, and Asa Hodges.[12] Under their leadership, the legislature passed several comprehensive bills, the most important of which was Act 19, the registration bill.[13] This act immediately became the major link in the chain which made Governor Powell Clayton the complete master of Arkansas. This chain of power also included the governor's unlimited appointive power, his power of appointment and dismissal of registrars, and the radical voters with their suffrage in the hands of the registrars. No break from these four links appeared in sight, because the leaders of the radical voters were appointed to jobs, probably two thousand in all.

The registration act controlled by the governor was a cruel one. The registrars and all board members were to be appointed by the governor and subject to his removal. They had total discretion to register or not register voters and to remove them from the rolls. A mistreated citizen could only apply to the Arkansas Supreme Court, which few people would do. The only thing Clayton lacked was the power to enforce his wishes even upon his enemies. That power was to be a strong militia.

FOOTNOTES

[1] Section 10 of Schedule of Constitution of 1868.

[2] Papers of the Historical Society of Delaware, No. XLI. *The Clayton Family*, Henry F. Hepburn, pp. 1 to 40, especially p. 20.

[3] Letter from Dale T. Kirkman to author, Phillips County Historical Society, August 5, 1975.

[4] Powell Clayton, *Aftermath of the Civil War*, page 14.

[5] *Arkansas Gazette*, July 3, 1868, 2-2.

[6] *Ibid.*, July 16, 1868, 2-2.

[7] Fayetteville *Democrat*, August 1, 1868, 2-7.

[8] *Republican*, July 21, 1868, 2-1.

[9] *Acts of Arkansas*, 1868, p. 148, Act. 48.

[10] *Arkansas Gazette*, January 11, 1923, and October 16, 1866, 2-1.

[11] George Hyman Thompson thesis, University of Arkansas Library, p. 264.

[12] Kelly Bryant, *Historical Report of the Secretary of State*, (Little Rock: 1968), pp. 329-330.

[13] *Acts of General Assembly of Arkansas*, 1868-9, p. 50, approved July 15, 1868. Fort Smith *Herald*, August 10, 1872.

Chapter 3

The Militia — "Damn You, You Didn't Vote Right."

After the General Assembly adjourned on July 23, 1868, Clayton instructed R.F. Catterson to organize the militia.* Few whites joined, and the result was a militia made up primarily of blacks, then unemployed, vagrants, and criminals. Whites trembled at the thought of a militia made up of the worst of their former slaves, even though the officers were whites who had formerly served in the Union Army or were stragglers who followed the army south. People fearfully saw the recruits drilling and watched to see where they would strike first.

Numerous incidents of violence erupted around the state over a period of several months. They were widely reported in the forty-odd newspapers of the state, almost half of which were Republican. Many of the reports were conflicting. The following pages describe some of the worst incidents of that time — events which Clayton used to justify his militia attacks.

In Conway County, fifty miles northwest of Little Rock, trouble began over a trivial matter.[1] Three black radicals threatened an ex-Confederate blackman at his home. The Confederate's dog barked, and the attackers shot the dog. The radicals were tried, but a black radical refused to serve on a jury with a black conservative. The trial ended, but the two groups of blacks armed themselves and fought each other.[2] The radicals also threatened Lewisburg (now Morrilton).

---

* We know little about Catterson prior to this date. The Public Service Administration failed to locate any military record. In Arkansas, he had the reputation of a bully.

27

Two whites, Thomas Burchfield and Thomas Bentley, went from Lewisburg among the blacks to assess the trouble, and Burchfield was killed. Dr. Nimrod Menifee, a man respected by both races, accompanied several others to assure the armed blacks that the rumors that the whites planned to take the blacks' property and drive them away were merely the fabrications of trouble-makers. Some people speculated that John Gibbons, later a radical militia officer, and James Hinds, a radical Representative in Congress, had stirred up the freedmen. There were no other known causes of this trouble.

Clayton wanted to show his fairness, and about ten days later, on August 27, 1868, the governor took Augustus H. Garland, Sandy Faulkner, and W.D. Blocker, all prominent conservatives, to Lewisburg on the steamboat *Hesper*. They brought temporary peace to the town. On the 29th, both the governor and Garland spoke to the blacks, who outnumbered the whites, counseled forbearance, and advised the freedmen to go home.[3]

The *New York Times* repeated a story from the *Dallas County Standard* of August 29 that a real battle occurred at Lewisville in Lafayette County, in which five whites and seven blacks were killed. A black man committed a horrible crime upon a 13-year-old white girl and the whites hanged him. The black's brother came to town and lectured and insulted the whites at length, and the whites hanged him also. Then about sixty blacks took up the fight, resulting in the twelve deaths.[4]

The November general election was in the offing, and a Democratic committee composed of Garland, U.M. Rose, and S.L. Tucker, members of the Little Rock Democratic Club, asked Clayton for fairness in the appointment of registration and election commissioners. The governor said he had already appointed the registrars and could not remove any of them.

The group asked him to send instructions to the registrars that would guarantee a fair election, but Clayton refused on the ground that as an executive he could not interfere with the judicial decisions of the registrars. When the committee pointed out that he had already sent them instructions, he replied that he had only told them what the law was.[5]

In late September the conservative leaders, fearful of losing future conflicts, advised obeying the law. They pointed to the speeches of Clayton and Garland at Lewisburg. Clayton had pledged fair elections, fair and impartial administration of the laws, and fair registrations. The conservatives stated, "We therefore sincerely recommend to our people in every possible way to uphold and preserve the public peace and to quietly await the verdict of the American people in the coming election, Grant vs. Seymour for president." The statement signed by Daniel Ringo, George E. Watkins, E.H. English, William Woodruff, U.M. Rose, Sandy Faulkner, C.M. Taylor, Gordon Peay, and other leaders.[6] The conservative leadership wanted a quiet Arkansas, and all evidence indicates they succeeded.

This signed statement was probably inspired by another one signed at the health resort at White Sulphur Springs, West Virginia, on the previous August 28. It, too, pledged obedience to the law and fairness to the freedmen and was signed by General Robert E. Lee; Alexander H. Stephens, ex-President of the Confederacy; Confederate General P.T.G. Beauregard; and men from eight former states of the Confederacy. Similar statements followed over the South.

In actual practice, the registration law proved more unjust than at first anticipated. Voting against the adoption of the constitution of 1868 was often used as an excuse for refusing to register an applicant, and other equally unjust excuses were used including close kinship to a conservative. The state had about 80,000 men of voting age, of whom 50,000 were white Southerners. Even though Arkansas' population was only 25 per cent black, blacks registered 22,000 against 33,000 whites.[7] This registration system caused the conservatives to lose several elections. President Johnson, on Christmas Day, 1868, pardoned all ex-Confederates except about 200 who were disqualified by the Fourteenth Amendment, but the people of Arkansas were for years oppressed by this state registration system and the vast powers of the registrars. The governor's power to appoint or remove the registrars was his second greatest weapon in controlling elections.

On September 19 Simpson Mason, radical registrar of Fulton County, who had been an Arkansas Unionist and had been accused of murdering several people, was ambushed and killed, probably by his conservative enemies.[8] At that point, the militia had not been properly organized and was not needed. Colonel William Monks, a Civil War Union officer who had his organized followers in Missouri, immediately came down from Western Grove with a squad of followers to exact revenge.[9] Monks and his men captured a number of prisoners.

Elisha Baxter, an Arkansas Unionist who had been appointed circuit judge by Clayton, wrote Monks:

> We ask you most earnestly, as officially representing the Judiciary of Arkansas, to turn over these persons [prisoners he had taken] to the sheriff. We beg of you as citizens, to allow the

majesty of the law to be vindicated in this matter, and not to imperil the lives and homes and property of all good citizens of the state.[10]

Baxter wrote this letter from the Fulton County Court, which was then in session, and proceeded to issue a writ of habeas corpus, which Monks obeyed. The whole incident demonstrated that the law could work even against dangerous men.

While sending these prisoners to the care of the court, someone ambushed and killed Uriah Bush, the strongest suspect in the murder of Simpson Mason. Admittedly this was a radical murder, but friends of Bush claimed that Mason had murdered Bush's child. The *Gazette* severely criticized Baxter for the courteous language of this letter to someone the paper considered to be an outlaw.[11]

Apparently Monks and his crew returned later to help in further militia activities. Monks was considered a criminal by his enemies and a patriot by his friends.[12] In either case, he was definitely a radical guerilla.

The Fulton County people organized an effective army for defense. Some Arkansas leaders felt Clayton was inspired to organize the militia because of the murder of Mason. However, a close look at the troubles of the times shows that the militia was organized by Clayton to ensure his complete political domination of Arkansas. All criminal cases should have been handled by state and federal officers, as General Smith had recommended to Clayton.[13]

During Clayton's term in office, the Ku Klux Klan began in Tennessee a little earlier and spread rapidly over the southeastern states. The Klan was never strong in Arkansas, but Clayton saw in the organization the possibility of a scapegoat or an excuse to persecute the people of Arkansas. Clayton became obsessed with blaming the Klan for every unfortunate incident which occurred.

In 1914, Clayton published his memoirs, *Aftermath of the Civil War*. In the book he told how he sent paid spies into about a dozen counties to infiltrate the Klan and keep him abreast of the group's activities. That was dangerous business, and A.H. Parker was detected in White County and executed. His body was thrown in a well where it was discovered later. Two prominent citizens, Jacob Frolich and Dandridge McRae, were indicted as accessories after the fact. Both men fled the state and remained absent about two years. They returned in the summer of 1871 and were found "not guilty" although they probably knew about the murder. This was one of the more brutal acts of the Klan. Otherwise the Ku Klux Klan had little influence in Arkansas.[14]

Confederate General Hindman was shot through the window of his home in Helena and killed September 27, 1868.[15] The radical press suggested that the enemies Hindman made in Arkansas during the war committed the crime, and that his wife, a sister of Cameron Biscoe, had planned a suit for divorce, causing Biscoe to shoot Hindman. This story was published so quickly that it appeared to the conservatives to be a coverup to shield the real killer, and the charges were hotly denied. Clayton in his memoirs insisted that a Memphis attorney would have filed the divorce suit had Hindman not been killed. Biscoe called the divorce story a lie in the St. Louis *Dispatch* and the denial was reprinted in the *Gazette*.[16]

The tracks of the murders showed that two men committed the crime, which suggests it was an organized affair and not the act of one disappointed man.[17]

Before the war, Hindman had been a spirited political campaigner with few equals. A capable speaker, he was instrumental in leading Arkansas into secession. In 1862 while the Federals under General Curtis were pushing toward Little Rock from Helena, he ordered a scorched earth policy. Under his orders, eleven whites and one black were executed to secure obedience to the Confederate cause.[18] Thus Hindman had enemies who could have committed the crime, the radicals argued.

Hindman went to Mexico after the war and immediately sided with Maximillian, brother of Emperor Francis Joseph of Austria. Maximillian, with some support from Napoleon III of France, wanted to make himself Emperor of Mexico. As soon as the Civil War ended, the United States let it be known that it sided with Mexico, and Maximillian lost support rapidly. Therefore, Hindman again found himself in trouble. Hearing that the United States was not executing ex-Confederate generals, he returned and secured a pardon.

Because he was a capable and determined organizer, Hindman by 1868 was rising rapidly as a leading opponent of the radicals. On April 5 Clayton and Hindman met in a heated debate at Helena, and at Searcy on August 15. Hindman attacked the opposition at length with abusive language and ended his speech by saying, "He who dallies is a dastard, and he who doubts is doomed."[19] No help came from the governor in finding the killer. The murder remains unsolved.

The *Gazette* of October 18 published another example of these atrocities — an article from the *Monticellonian* of the 10th, which related how W.O. Dollar, a deputy, and a black man, Fred Reeves, were both shot and their bodies tied together, as if kissing face to face, and left lying in the street. They were pronounced bad men by the Monticello authorities, and Stokley Morgan was executed for this crime.

Governor Clayton wanted better arms for the militia. After several failures, James L. Hodges and George R. Weeks obtained 5,000 muskets at Detroit. The guns were shipped to Memphis on the steamboat, *Belle Memphis*, but the White River Packet Company refused to take them to Arkansas. The arms reached Memphis about October 5, and the cargo and destination were noted in the Memphis papers. Since no transportation was available to take the guns to Arkansas they were unloaded on the wharf, guarded by the police, and later stored in a warehouse. Clayton had guaranteed to buy the arms, and he sent the steamboat *Hesper* to retrieve them. The guns were properly loaded on October 15. While the *Hesper* was taking on wood down river about 20 miles from Memphis, the steam tug *Nettie Jones* came aside. Armed and masked men boarded the *Hesper* and after moving the ship out in the stream they threw the guns in the muddy waters of the Mississippi River. They reboarded their own tug and steamed away.[20] The press reported that the governor again secured arms from a government arsenal in Detroit but had trouble getting a boat to bring them to Arkansas from a railroad terminal.[21]

Clayton was angered not only by the loss of his guns but also allegedly by the loss of profit which he, Hodges, Weeks, and several others expected to make from selling the guns to the state. According to the *Gazette* the invoices were altered to show $35,000 instead of the actual cost of about $17,000.[22] Clayton wired the Secretary of War, J.M. Schofield,[23] stating that the seizures of the arms was evidence of armed resistance in the state and asked for federal arms, then stored in Little Rock.

In his diary, Gideon Welles, Secretary of the Navy under Lincoln and Johnson, commented on the cabinet meeting concerning Clayton's request for arms, that opinions were divided until [Secretary of War] Schofield read a telegram from a Colonel Campbell of the Federal troops at Little Rock, stating that "it was not expedient to listen to or to be governed by representations of the governor." The tone then changed, and the arms were not sent. A few days later, Clayton published a circular to the presidents of the registration boards stating that he could not send the requested troops to enforce the registration laws, and that the governor wanted the upcoming 1868 presidential election to be a "free and open election."[24] Clayton had wanted arms for his militia not U.S. troops.

On October 22, 1868, Joseph Brooks and James Hinds were riding to Indiana Bay in eastern Monroe County for a political rally. Both men were radicals who had been prominent in the Constitutional Convention that year, and Hinds was the U.S. representative from District Three, which stretched from Little Rock to the northwest corner of Arkansas. The *Republican*, the leading radical paper, reported that George W. Clark, chairman of the Democratic Central Committee of Monroe County, rode up to Hinds and began talking to him.[25] Hinds was riding a considerable distance behind Brooks. Clark fired on Brooks with a double-barreled shotgun, sprinkling both horse and rider. Brooks said he turned and saw Clark fire the second barrel directly at Hinds, who fell mortally wounded. Although Brooks was not seriously wounded and rode away to seek help, no effort was made to arrest anyone. Hinds' body was brought to the Capitol in Little Rock where it lay in state for a day.[26]

No one ascertained why Brooks was riding safely ahead of his comrade when friendly men generally rode together. Even though Brooks claimed to have been wounded, no evidence remains of medical attention or any delay in his activities. The murder conveniently eliminated from competition with Clayton one of the leading contenders for the black vote. Neither Clark nor anyone else was ever brought to trial for this crime, although Clayton, having appointed all court officers and sheriffs, could have encouraged an investigation. The *Gazette* suggested the motive for the murder might have been to excite people in the North to support the radicals and improve Grant's chances for winning the Presidency on November 3.[27]

No George W. Clark appears on the census records of Monroe County for either 1860 or 1870 or on the deed records. The name George W. Clark does appear on a petition with 69 others asking the radical General Assembly to determine the boundaries of Monroe County, which was done in April, 1869. This name also appears in a book of names at the county courthouse in Clarendon, but the book refers to nothing.[28] There is practically no other trace of this man in the county.

A few days before Clayton's inauguration in late June, 1868, the General Assembly attempted to distribute heavily populated black counties among several congressional districts to insure the election of radical Representatives to Congress. The legislature abandoned the project when someone pointed out that the move would also help Hinds in his race for Congress.[29] Hinds' standing among the radicals had declined greatly and even though he was a radical and an agitator among blacks, he was nobody's stooge.[30] The *Gazette* recognized in him some fine qualities and suggested had Hinds lived he probably would have changed.

Harrell in *The Brooks-Baxter War*, strongly suggests that Hinds, though a persistent advocate of the rights of the freedmen, had fallen out with the radicals' attempts to govern Arkansas and reported that Hinds told him:

> I am going to the country for few days, and I devote the establishment [the Powell Clayton machine] to the infernal gods ... Yes, these fellows have builded upon my foundation; they have reaped what I have sown. They plant a little whirlwind for me now and they shall reap a cyclone. I am a cyclone producer ... and they know it.[31]

Strangely, the press, especially the radical papers, said little about this entire affair. Brooks and Hinds had often traveled together to meetings of blacks. Hinds tried to teach the freedmen their political rights, and Brooks would follow with a talk showing the relationship of religion to politics. The ex-Confederates had little regard for either Brooks or Hinds, and Powell Clayton probably classified both men as dangerous competitors for the black vote and consequently for the control of Arkansas.

No one can say what kind of man Hinds would have made had he lived. He had some good qualities, was honest and courteous, but understood nothing of Southern life. His death had some markings of a killing from within the radical ring.[32]

On October 27, 1868, Governor Clayton stretched the powers given him in the 1868 registration law and by proclamation decreed that, due to lawlessness, no election would be held on November 3 in the counties of Ashley, Bradley, Columbia, Hot Spring, Lafayette, Mississippi, Woodruff, Sharp, Craighead, Sevier, and Green. Little trouble had occurred in these heavily conservative counties, and Clayton expected to guarantee the Northern radicals a Grant victory in Arkansas.

But another incident demonstrates how much reports of this era sometimes conflicted. Elisha Baxter, the judge in the Third Judicial Circuit, had been active in encouraging the people of his circuit to obey the law. In mid-December, he presided over a nonpartisan meeting at Batesville which 500 people attended. Baxter advised the crowd to uphold the law, and no trouble occurred there. As a result, General D.P. Upham left Batesville with his militia and went to Augusta where the Ku Klux Klan had held a parade in the early part of the month. Edward W. Thompson, a federal captain, formerly from Maine, who served as Baxter's acting prosecuting attorney, became embroiled in a controversy.

The *Arkansas Gazette* said on Saturday, November 28, 1868:
> ... Mr. E. W. Thompson having been knocked down in a bar room in this town [Batesville] on Saturday night last [one week before] is recovering. He states he does not know who did it

...the whole thing was a drunken spree, Mr. Thompson being drunk.

But the New York *Times*, on the 27th, one day earlier, stated that Thompson had "been shot and mortally wounded by persons who took offense at his voting for Grant."[33]

The available evidence indicates that Thompson was succeeded as acting prosecuting attorney by W.A. Inman on the following December 8. In 1877 Elisha Baxter (who in the meantime had served as governor) even took Thompson as a law partner and Thompson appeared in a few legal cases. He actually died at Batesville eleven years later on December 19, 1879, fathering three children after his supposedly mortal wound.

Both sides published truthful papers but the *Republican* was not always one of them. It was primarily partisan — a propaganda sheet. For example, Stephen Wheeler, Senator from White County, was involved in many radical operations. In August someone shot him in the arm[34] but the wound was slight and Wheeler lost no time convalescing. The *Republican*, however, immediately reported Wheeler's assassination and never corrected the story.

On November 4, 1868, the conflict between the radicals and conservatives culminated in Powell Clayton's declaration of martial law in the counties of Ashley, Bradley, Columbia, Craighead, Greene, Lafayette, Little River, Mississippi, Sevier, and Woodruff.[35] Later, the governor added other counties. Clayton claimed in his message to the General Assembly of November 24 that several murders of Union men and other atrocities had occurred in these counties. Clayton never substantiated these reports. Conservatives speculated that Clayton declared martial law because most of the counties voted against the radicals in previous elections.[36]

In mid-November, after Grant's election, the governor sent a letter to all county officials, and from Memphis wired a copy to the New York *Times*:

> The election now over, the time has now arrived when the state government must sustain itself at the point of a bayonet, if necessary. The American people have by overwhelming majorities [election of November 3, 1868 in which Grant was elected President] declared in favor of the validity of the reconstruction measures and the government set up under the United States authorities. In deference to the decisions of the people we ask no help from abroad... The enemies of the state government are demoralized by the stunning blow received on the third inst... [Grant's victory].
>
> You are requested to perfect an organization of the militia in your county. If the loyal people do not volunteer in the state

guard, reserve militia must be organized. When called upon, you must furnish your quota of militia to operate in other portions of the state and urge upon the citizens not to act upon their own opinions against the authorities. A general plan is agreed upon.[37]

Clayton apparently intended this letter primarily for Northern consumption, because the governor had already dispatched militia to some counties.

The counties selected for attack had large white population and their leading towns lacked influential newspapers like those of Little Rock, Fort Smith, Helena, Fayetteville and Pine Bluff. The designated counties were inhabited by the poorer and most conservative whites and had the greatest number of Klan members. In short, the governor picked them because of their opposition to the radical program.

Clayton claimed he summoned the militia because the Ku Klux Klan was ravaging those counties and killing loyal men of both races.

Almost no publicity was given to the recruitment of this militia, and some of them, if not all, were drilled when no one likely would be there. The enabling Act No. 18 was approved by Governor Clayton July 16, 1868. It stated that every male of the state able to serve could be called except public officials, those made ineligible by the laws of the United States, and some smaller classes. Others could be excused by paying $5 per year.

Ex-Confederates or their sympathizers surely were not wanted in any attacks upon white commanders. Former slaves, the unemployed, and criminals were naturals. No doubt such elements were easily recruited.

The 1868 presidential election contributed to the beginning of militia activities in Arkansas. The radicals considered it rather unpatriotic for Southern people to vote against General Grant and the same counties which were heavily white and had voted against the constitution of 1868 had also voted against the new president. When the militia arrested a white man and the man asked what he was charged with, often militiamen replied, "Damn you, you didn't vote right."

The militia hit hardest in the counties that voted most heavily for Seymour, the Democratic presidential candidate. Little River County voted 227 for Seymour and 20 for Grant; Woodruff County 1407 for Seymour and 39 for Grant; and Hempstead County, near Center Point, 1325 for Seymour and 33 for Grant. According to the 1860 census these counties had a high percentage (75 per cent or more) of white people and therefore the most Klan members. But they also had the highest level of education and the most human treatment over the years for the freedmen, for low black population has always resulted in racial peace.

Nevertheless, the *Arkansas Gazette* on November 8, 1868, asked the Arkansas people to accept Grant's election graciously; "Remember his good treatment of Lee and his good report as regarding Southern people as indicative of his ability to be a good President. Do not hurt the South by resistance or rebellion." Many Southerners bore patiently the atrocities in hopes that Grant would change things when he became president on March 4, 1869. On December 1, the *Gazette* again cautioned people to submit.

But Clayton took advantage of the situation. The governor claimed that the Ku Klux Klan perpetrated all crimes.[38] However, some of the major crimes were committed in counties other than the ones attacked by the militia. The targeted counties were concentrated in the northeast, southeast and southwest sections. On November 18, Keyes Danforth, Clayton's secretary, announced the appointment of three militia generals: Robert F. Catterson for the southwest corner, D.P. Upham for the northeast, and Sam Mallory for the southeast.[39] They were to command the troops and occupy the counties in each district in which martial law had been declared. The northwest corner, though declared a district, was left alone, except for Conway County.

The governor ordered the militia to live off the assigned territory. Upon arrival at the main town of a county, militia officials reportedly demanded the keys to stores, rifled the cash drawers, looted the stores of more goods than they could take home, got drunk, burned some buildings, and killed a few armed men who would not submit.[40] Several women allegedly were raped during the militia campaign, and the militiamen stole hogs, chickens, cattle and work stock. Liquor and gun stores were supposedly favorite targets. Conflicting reports have appeared on some incidents.[41] The victims, in their reports to the press, described these events in such brutal terms that they are hard to believe. On the other side, the militia and the radical press spoke of gallant leaders, glorious victory, and final triumph over brutal rebels and the Klan.

On November 10, Catterson staged a sneak attack on Center Point in Howard County.[42] His objectives included the capture of Cullen Baker, a desperado who operated in northeast Texas and in southwest Arkansas. Baker was a professional killer who had no association with the political situation in the state.

Following the initial attack on November 10, the militia returned the next day, arresting many local men and herding them into a field while the remainder of the militia rifled the stores. Eventually Catterson's forces shot several Center Point men.[43] One young man named Willingham secured a gun, killed one militiaman and wounded several others before he was killed.[44]

The attack on Center Point took the community by surprise and was unexpectedly harsh because the militia arrived before the news of the declaration of martial law. The only justification ever offered for the raid was the charge that the citizens had voted against the radicals. Nearly all reports from southwest Arkansas were similar to the Center Point incident. The uncontrolled militiamen apparently sacked communities, stole horses, raped women, and killed at least eight men.[45]

Estimates indicated that the number of horses and mules taken by the militia from the people in the Center Point and Paraclift communities ranged from 300 to 500. Since the 1868 Constitution said, "Private property shall not be taken for public use without just compensation therefor," the militia did issue some receipts. Stephen Wheeler, quartermaster general, published an advertisement in several papers on January 20, 1869, serving notice that people holding receipts and proving ownership within 10 days could reclaim horses, mules, saddles, and bridles. But the conditions of transportation made it unlikely that many victims could successfully reclaim their property by the deadline.[46] On February 19, Wheeler advertised the unclaimed stock for sale.

By November 22, Catterson's first report appeared in the Little Rock papers. They had killed eight men, mostly at Center Point. The report continues: "Strongly pickuted (sic), our camp barriacaded and the men in good spirits, officials [white] well, plenty to eat, and in good fighting order, if fighting necessary.

"There could be no doubt of us being taken for anything but state troops, for the fact that the United States flag was carried, and cavalry guidons."

One can forgive the United States flag and the cavalry guidons; they are inanimate. The flag was a poor notice that innocent people were to be shot down, for the American flag heretofore had been considered a sign of protection, not assassination. For food, they foraged, and surely they told the truth about having plenty.

In early February Senator Sam Mallory (who had been also a militia general) pushed an appropriation bill in the Senate to pay militia expenses of about $85,000.

Senator J.C. Ray of Clark County, representing the southwestern section, objected and asked, "Where did they meet an enemy?" to which Mallory replied, "At Center Point."

Ray denied that the militia ever came in "contact with any body of men who were opposing the execution of civil law," and Mallory replied, "One militiaman [was] killed at Center Point." An angry Ray, after stating that the militia had killed eight unarmed citizens commented, "It was the most dishonorable outrage ever committed on a civilized people."[47]

Mr. Ray's name appears no more on the rolls of the successive General Assemblies.

About the same time that Catterson reached Center Point, Captain J.E. Tourtellotte of the U.S. Infantry arrived in Little River County on November 11 with a company of thirty men to investigate the killing near the Louisiana border of P.J. Andrews and H.E. Willis, employees of the Freedmen's Bureau. The captain verified that the two men had been murdered, but his investigation failed to identify the killers. Tourtellotte, who had been sent by the federal army and not Governor Clayton, reported no conditions justifying the actions of the militia. In fact, he noted the local response to the militia:

The excitement and threats on the part of the Negro militia, above referred to, have caused much prejudice against the Negro militia and perhaps the militia generally, and people fear further outbreaks.[48]

In 1914 J.D. Demby, a former militia officer, wrote a defense of the Center Point affair at Clayton's request. He said the militia encountered the Klan, armed and ready for battle. According to Demby, part of the Klan fled down a road, and the militia feigned a strike in front but swung to the rear and killed eight Klansmen. This story conflicts with other reports, including Catterson's. Yet Clayton repeated it in his book published a month before his death in 1914.

FOOTNOTES

[1] *Arkansas Gazette*, August 28, 1868, 3-2.

[2] *Ibid.*, August 29, 1868, 3-2.

[3] *Ibid.*, September 9, 1868, 2-1.

[4] *Ibid.*, September 2, 1868, 1-2. This same story was also found in the Memphis *Daily Appeal*.

[5] *Ibid.*, September 18, 1868, 2-2.

[6] Memphis *Daily Appeal*, September 22, 1868, 2-3.

[7] John Ferguson and J. H. Atkinson, *Historic Arkansas*, (Little Rock: Arkansas History Commission, 1966), p. 149.

[8] *Arkansas Gazette*, September 25, 1868, 2-1; October 1, 1868, 2-2, and December 21, 1868, 2-1.

[9] New York *Times*, October 2, 1868, 3-3.

[10] *Arkansas Gazette*, September 25, 1868, 2-1, and October 11, 1868, 1-2.

[11] *Ibid.*, October 7, 1868, 2-1, and October 11, 1868, 1-2.

[12] *Ibid.*, August 3, 1870, 3-1.
[13] *Ibid.*, September 25, 1868, 2-1.
[14] *Ibid.*, September 10, 1868, and September 1, 1871, 1-2.
[15] *Ibid.*, September 29, 1868, 2-2, and October 11, 1868, 1-2.
[16] *Ibid.*, December 1, 1868, 1-2.
[17] Memphis *Daily Appeal*, October 6, 1868, 1-3.
[18] *Arkansas Gazette*, August 6, 1866, 1-3.
[19] *Ibid.*, October 6, 1868.
[20] Memphis *Daily Appeal*, October 17, 1868, 3-2, and October 26, 1868, 2-2. And New York *Times*, October 17, 1868, 1-5.
[21] New York *Times*, October 17, 1868, 1-5.
[22] *Arkansas Gazette*, August 14, 1871, 2-1.
[23] New York *Times*, November 18, 1879, 1-4.
[24] *Ibid.*, October 26, 1868, 2-6.
[25] *Arkansas Gazette*, October 24, 1868, 3-2, and October 21, 1868, 2-2; and New York *Times*, October 26, 1868, 2-6.
[26] *Arkansas Gazette*, October 25, 1868, 2-2, and October 28, 1868, 3-2.
[27] *Ibid.*, October 1869, 2-1.
[28] Monroe County records thoroughly checked by author September 1970.
[29] *Republican*, June 30, 1868, 2-2.
[30] New York *Times*, October 30, 1868, 2-6.
[31] Harrell, pp. 40-41.
[32] Personal investigations of the author in Woodruff County in September 1979.
[33] New York *Times*, October 27, 1868, 1-2. (The headline was "Murder of District Attorney in Arkansas.")
[34] *Arkansas Gazette*, August 18, 1868, 2-1.
[35] *Ibid.*, November 6, 1868, 2-1.
[36] *Journal of Senate of Arkansas*, 1868-69, pp. 280-295.
[37] New York *Times*, November 18, 1868, 1-2.
[38] Fort Smith *Tri-Weekly Herald*, September 5, 1871.
[39] *Arkansas Gazette*, November 18, 1868, 2-1.
[40] *Ibid.*, October 21, 1868, 2-1.
[41] New York *Times*, October 25, 1868, 11-3. *Arkansas Gazette*, November 22, 1868, 2-2.
[42] *Democrat*, December 5, 1868.
[43] *Arkansas Democrat*, December 5, 1868.
[44] *Arkansas Gazette*, January 14, 1869, 1-2.
[45] Memphis *Daily Appeal*, November 11, 1868, 2-3.
[46] *Arkansas Gazette*, November 20, 1869, 2-6.
[47] *Ibid.*, February 7, 1869, 2-3.
[48] *Ibid.*, November 29, 1868, 1-3.

Chapter 4

A Waste-Howling Wilderness

The General Assembly began its work of the second session of 1868 on November 23, when quorums in both houses were present for the first time. That same day, Joseph Brooks, representative from Phillips County, introduced a resolution approving Clayton's action in declaring martial law and sending forth the militia.[1] The atrocity at Center Point was just then reaching the press. Brooks made one of the most impassioned speeches of his career, thanking "God that the rebel Philistines had again been visited with the lightning of His terrible swift sword."[2]

Reverend Brooks had had several bitter experiences since the war began. Like most influential Unionists, he speculated in cotton but lost his profits at New Orleans. He also lost a brother, Colonel William Brooks, commander of the company of federal troops at Helena.

Perhaps the *Gazette* was more than a little facetious the next day in describing Brooks' speech as "a seriousness of manner absolutely ludicrous," and describing him, "with swollen veins, menacing gesticulations, and hair standing out like quills upon a fretful porcupine."[3] Brooks spoke of marching bands of rebels, the Klan, and the need to enforce the laws or make Arkansas a wasteland from the Missouri line to the Red River "until we shall not have a habitation here, except for moles and bats." Although the expression "marching bands of rebels and Klan" was used many times by radicals in their reports, the Arkansas press reported only one march, a peaceful one, at Augusta.

"I hope," Brooks said in his oration, "we shall adopt the resolution ... That, sir is what we want; and that is what we will have; we will have peace; we will have enforcement of the laws, freedom of speech, and the press and protection of life and property — or we will have a waste-howling wilderness."4 Brooks drew his metaphor from Deuteronomy. His remarks were remembered as his "waste-howling wilderness" speech and have been quoted and misquoted many times since. His resolution carried 69 to 0. Brooks appeared to be trying to become Clayton's main ally or perhaps make himself the leading radical in Hinds' absence. Brooks spoke in favor of the militia activities well in January, 1869.5

The *Gazette* described him as:
JOE BROOKS, THE BIBLE BANGER
Imagine a man of five feet eleven, brawny and bony, built like a Conestoga, with a face the hue and hardness of a pine knot, and a pair of staring eyeballs of the same hue and hardness, high cheek bones and mouth with teeth standing apart, incessantly grins horribly a ghastle smile, who was up on every question presented to the House, and you have Joe Brooks, the Bible Banger.6

Like Brooks, Governor Clayton's message to the General Assembly on November 24 stressed lawlessness, murder, and marching Klansmen. He also advocated disfranchising the ex-Confederates:

When this class of people show a willingness to recognize and acquiesce fully in the measures, and support the government established hereby [Clayton's government] it will be time enough to take into consideration their enfranchisement.7

After Clayton's address, the militia continued its work, although Mallory did less damage in the southeast than the militia in the other two sections. However, Catterson did sack the county seat of Ashley County, where five federal soldiers were murdered in 1867. Drew County, north of Ashley, had voted heavily against Grant and the constitution of 1868 and therefore became a target.

Although Drew County was the site of an atrocity and voted 40 to 1 against Grant, Mallory hesitated in taking punitive action. Drew County was populous and had close ties to influential people and a newspaper that might publicize any atrocities. Monticello, relatively unscarred by the war, had the remnents of pre-war wealth, and the residents may have literally bought some peace. S.A. Duke, a wealthy and influential Monticello carpetbagger who soon became a state senator, had a calming influence on Mallory. As senator, he later voted with the native Southerners against severe punitive measures.

Militia Captain Prigmore of Pine Bluff drilled about 200 black men and brought them to Monticello November 30 in advance of

Mallory. Disorder broke out in the form of broken doors and windows, drinking, and fighting. Eventually two leading citizens named Jackson and Berks assembled about 200 well-armed volunteers. They disarmed many of the militia and restored order, with help from Mallory. Mallory advised Prigmore to take the unit back to the camp and they left the next morning but sacked the defenseless village of Relf's Bluff on the way.[8]

The behavior of Carter McClelland at Monticello was noteworthy. He was born a slave about 1840, the son of his mother's owner. He joined the Confederate Army with his father, who was killed in Georgia in 1864. He then returned to Warren, a few miles west of Monticello, and joined Prigmore's militia.[9] McClelland was farsighted enough to realize that the conservative whites had sufficient strength to eventually win the skirmish at Monticello. Before the volunteers reached town, McClelland encouraged the troublemakers in the militia to be peaceful. He later did the same thing in Chicot County. He soon lived in Little Rock and supported Joseph Brooks.

Daniel P. Upham's militia in the northeast proved to be even more ruthless than Catterson's. Because of Elisha Baxter's efforts for peace in Independence County, Upham headed for Augusta in Woodruff County where the militia began jailing and murdering people. Upham's forces jailed John Thorp, Dr. M.D.L. McKenzie, B.Z. Jones, and a Mr. Ruddock, and then shot them and threw their bodies in the White River.[10] Major C.W. McCrary surrendered to Upham and was imprisoned. McCrary contracted pneumonia in the cold jail, but the militia refused to give him medical aid. Friends begged to take McCrary to a private residence for proper care. The militia finally granted their request about two hours before the prisoner died. Three black militiamen called James T. Bland from his home and blew off half of his head with a gun. For this act and two other unsuccessful murder attempts, their captain was promoted to Assistant Adjutant General.

During Upham's campaign, a number of businessmen escaped from Augusta to Memphis and several of them issued affidavits and statements concerning the militia's property destruction, stealing of merchants' stocks, and murder. They also claimed that the provost marshal of the militia company had demanded $5,000 to leave the people alone. He sent collectors around Woodruff County getting $100 to $500 to be unmolested. Since Woodruff County was then poorly developed, the militia attacked the residents viciously.[11] According to an editorial in the *Arkansas Gazette* on January 5, 1869, the Upham militia grew to over 1,000 men, who lay around the camp in complete disregard of order, with no drilling. Heavy pickets surrounded them, and foragers were constantly going out in every direction and returning with stolen provisions. The governor finally withdrew the militia in late January.

Upham came to Arkansas from New York after failing in business. Alexander Shaler, who sold the business to Upham, also left New York and eventually became the commander of the federal cavalry post at De Vall's Bluff, Arkansas. A federal draft dodger, Upham secretly visited Shaler in March, 1865. He secured the rights to operate saloons and buy cotton, which were activities under federal military supervision. Northern investors gave Upham a half interest in saloons for acquiring these rights from Shaler. Even though Upham had less than ten dollars in his pockets when he located Shaler, by July he had a one-fourth interest in a 2,000-acre leased cotton plantation, a half interest in the best saloon in De Vall's Bluff, a half interest in the only saloon at the cavalry depot where federal soldiers could drink, a half interest in a steamboat trade, sole ownership of a saloon in Augusta, and a saloon in Jacksonport.

The boat trade was another profitable venture during the war. Confederate authorities had tried to destory cotton to prevent its falling into Union hands, but the people hid thousands of bales. After the Confederacy fell in the spring of 1865, these same people bought supplies with cotton. Upham's boat company charged 25 cents, or a pound of cotton, for goods that cost ten cents and sold the cotton for 50 cents or more.[12]

Daniel Upham eventually talked his brother Henry into coming to Arkansas, and the Woodruff County deed records show that they soon became substantial land owners. Land, the only item besides cotton which Southerners could convert into cash, sold cheaply. Upham rose overnight from a penniless draft dodger to a wealthy man and eventually became a general in Powell Clayton's militia. Cases like this occurred in the South over and over. Powell Clayton himself even acquired a large plantation southeast of Pine Bluff not long after settling in Arkansas.

Two other atrocities committed by the Upham militia deserve historical mention. Samuel Baker, a British officer, was traveling through Arkansas for his health. He had been wounded in the Battle of Sevastapol in the Crimean War and arrived at Searcy while the militia was fighting in Woodruff County. He left Searcy for Augusta, where he intended to take a steamboat north. When he saw the behavior of the militia at Augusta, he expressed his indignation and was summarily shot to death without a trial.[13] When news of this atrocity reached the Arkansas press, Upham produced three affidavits that Baker was a loud-mouthed drunkard who should have moved on but instead continued criticizing the militia and was shot to death by unknown parties.[14]

At that time Great Britain was beginning discussions with the United States about the Alabama claims. This claim involved federal ships destroyed during the Civil War by the ship Alabama and nine others which were built and armed in England. The United States eventually received $15,000,000 in gold. These negotiations prevented the British government from protesting Baker's death.[15]

In another incident, Upham's militia stole two black mules, one of them from B.J. Davis of Mississippi County. Davis and John B. Thorpe tried to recover the mules, but both men lost their lives, and one of the mules later appeared on Upham's farm. Joe Little, alledgedly on the militia's instructions, killed Davis. Little claimed he had immunity from prosecution, but the militia executed him on short notice, not even permitting him to see the priest he requested.[16]

The northern press, including the New York *Times*, sometimes printed false reports putting the radicals in a favorable light. However, as time passed, some papers changed their viewpoint. A good example was the New York *Tribune*, which had been founded and edited by Horace Greeley. Greeley had opposed slavery and secession and sympathized with the radicals after the war. He published radical letters and telegrams from the South, called President Andrew Johnson "the greatest criminal," and supported the election of Grant and Colfax in 1868. Shortly after the presidential election he published a charge that in Drew County, Arkansas, the Klan, the night before the election, whipped all prominent blacks almost to death and threatened to kill them if they did not vote for Seymour, thereby forcing about 700 to vote for the Democratic ticket. Those familiar with the rather quiet conditions of the county and its relatively favorable racial attitudes found this story rather dubious.

But by 1871 the attitude of the paper had changed. On May 1 the *Tribune* reported: "The fault [for Southern troubles] lies with a few wicked men . . . evils are the natural and inevitable result of its new relations. Slaves of yesterday are the masters of today. Violence and murder the natural consequence." The New York *Times* also changed.

In Conway County no trouble had occurred since Clayton, Garland, and others had quieted the situation in September. Sheriff N.W. Moore, a Unionist during the war, notified Clayton he could get enough local help and did not need the militia. However, on December 12, 1868, Clayton dispatched John J. Gibbons, a radical from Perry County, with a company of black militia, which began with a sacking of the Lewisburg business section. The troops burned Breeding, Billingsley, and Casey, the town's largest company, and the militia reported that Casey had been killed and his body burned in the fire. The fire spread to several buildings, including one belonging to two radicals, Gill and Matthews. Gibbons reported to the Governor that the conservatives must have burned that one. He also reported holding an inquiry which suggested that Breeding and Billinglsey killed Casey and ran off with the firm's money.[17] Later investigations indicated that all three partners were killed by the militia and their bodies burned to cover the theft of the cash.

These activites generated a growing opposition to the militia among legislators, especially Northwest Arkansas Unionists. A House resolution in January to approve of the militia activities lost 22 to 46. Clayton pressured the representatives and the measure then carried 55 to 13. Clayton was able to maintain his influence over the assembly through patronage and control of the election machinery.

The governor also counted on the support of several diehard loyalists. For example, Joseph Brooks actively supported the militia and Clayton's programs, including the refunding of the much disputed and infamous Holford bonds of the defunct State Real Estate Bank. This bond issue dated back to 1840, and the radicals frequently reminded Arkansas of this scandal as a defense for their own actions. The conservatives accused Brooks of receiving $25,000 for pushing the refunding plan through the General Assembly.[18] Despite Brooks' support, Clayton maintained a distance from him, and Brooks began moving away from the governor early in 1869. Clayton helped defeat Brooks for every position the legislator sought.

It is hard to understand how people could perform such brutal acts or atrocities as occurred on both sides. Revenge appears to have been the motive for many crimes. Southerners as well as Northerners committed crimes and atrocities, and neither side can escape blame. Archibald Napier and W. Maurice Williams, both natives of Polk County and Union soldiers, were successively appointed sheriff of Pope County. Napier was ambushed and killed in 1865, and Williams, his successor, met the same fate in 1866. Y.W. Etheridge, author of a history of Ashley County, wrote that the military director removed two county officials in 1867, and the people objected strenuously. Subsequently five soldiers stationed at the county seat were murdered while watering their horses and their bodies were thrown in the creek.[19]

Horace Greeley, who during the war worked hard for the freedom of the slaves, softened toward the South after the war and fought hard to prevent vengeful action. He was the first to sign the bond of Jefferson Davis, and was viciously criticized for doing so. Greeley wrote Senator Butler of Massachusetts, prominent among northern radicals, and encouraged him not to oppress the South. The editor of the *Tribune* especially objected to Butler's efforts to disfranchise ex-Confederates.[20] He said moderation was needed to gain support for the adoption of the Fifteenth Amendment to the Constitution, pointing out that several Northern states were rejecting the amendment. Greeley even used poetry in a second letter to make his point:

>Thank God that I have lived to see the time
>   When the great truth begins at last to find
>An utterance from the deep heart of mankind,
>   Earnest and clear, that all revenge is crime.[21]

But thousands of others fed on revenge. Wendell Phillips advocated a new and more complete conquest and annihilation of Southern conservatives.[22] The Southern people feared the reinvasion by the Federal Army and decided to suffer until Northern public opinion improved. When Congressional radicals passed the Enforcement Act, which prohibited state legislation denying citizens the right to vote because of race, color, or previous condition of servitude, some Southern whites objected.

In Arkansas, the activities of the militia continued to be a focus of conservative discontent. The Fayetteville *Democrat* of March 20, 1869, listed the cost of the militia to Arkansas as $140,000, but the citizens' property destroyed, stolen, or taken and receipted, was variously estimated from one to two million dollars. The paper also claimed around 50 people had been murdered.

In early 1869 the Arkansas General Assembly ordered a committee to report on militia behavior. Headed by Senator L.G. Barker of the Ninth District (Crittenden, St. Francis, and Woodruff Counties) a district fully under Clayton's control, the committee in early April gave the militia's performance a glowing report. Barker said there were about 2,000 militiamen in the state who were needed because the rebels had shot about 200 people in the five months prior to the declaration of martial law. He also reported the militia had executed many men for their crimes. The charge that the people of Arkansas had killed 200 people was repeated by the radicals after they were replaced in 1874, and the conservatives challenged them to bring the evidence before any grand jury. Clayton wrote his leaders in nearly every county in Arkansas to furnish names of those murdered, but there is no record of any response.

FOOTNOTES

[1] *Journal of the House*, 1868-69, p. 9.
[2] Harrel, p. 89.
[3] *Arkansas Gazette*, November 24, 1868, 2-1.
[4] *Ibid.*, November 24, 1868, 2-1.
[5] *Ibid.*, January 17, 1869, 2-2.
[6] *Ibid.*, February 19, 1869, 2-2.
[7] *Journal of Arkansas Senate*, 1868-69, pp. 280-295.
[8] Memphis *Daily Appeal*, January 10, 1869, 2-3.
[9] *Ibid.*, April 17, 1869, 3-2.
[10] *Arkansas Gazette*, January 17, 1869, 1-2, and Memphis *Daily Appeal*, December 15, 1868, 1-2, and December 18, 1868, 2-2.
[11] *Arkansas Gazette*, January 17, 1869.
[12] *Ibid.*, November 12, 1967, E 6-3, 4 & 5, and November 19, 1967, E 6-4, 5 & 6. Upham's letters to his brother Henry are in the *Gazette* archives.
[13] *Ibid.*, March 12, 1869, 2-1.
[14] Affidavits in Arkansas Historical Commission, Little Rock.
[15] *Arkansas Gazette*, December 20, 1868, 1-2.
[16] Memphis *Daily Appeal*, April 17, 1869, 4-3.
[17] *Arkansas Gazette*, December 22, 1868, 2-2, and January 8, 1869, 3-2.
[18] *Ibid.*, October 29, 1870.
[19] Y. W. Etheridge, *History of Ashley County, Arkansas* (Van Buren, Arkansas: The Press-Argus, 1959), pp. 109-120.
[20] *Arkansas Gazette*, December 4, 1869, 2-2.
[21] *Ibid.*, January 7, 1870, 3-1, 2 & 3.
[22] *Ibid.*, January 13, 1870, 2-2.

Chapter 5

An Independent Man Must Be Destroyed

On April 30, 1869, General C.H. Smith surrendered his authority over Arkansas under the Reconstruction Law.[1] He had been appointed in 1867 and had served impartially. He had also worked in Arkansas under the Freedman's Bureau between 1865 and 1867. He had been criticized in his appointment of registrars in 1867 because many were candidates for offices themselves. However, since the Reconstruction Acts required the appointment of Union supporters, officeholders were often the only Union supporters he could locate. The *Gazette* said, "In all other respects, we believe the administration of General Smith has been characterized by dignity, moderation, and efficiency." Perhaps some military tyrants were appointed in the South to administer the Reconstruction Acts, but not in Arkansas, nor did Arkansas ever have an essentially black government.

Had Clayton followed Smith's advice of allowing the federal marshals to arrest criminals and prosecute them in court,[2] most of the cruelties of the militia war might have been avoided. In some cases, federal officers campaigned for Southern candidates in elections. This prompted radical politicians to accuse the Southern people of playing to the military and making money off their cash trade. They did bring money, but the military did not fall for the radical dishonesty, and General Smith did object to Clayton's use of the militia.[3]

The militia's behavior eventually generated opposition to Clayton from within the Republican Party. His first opponent was John G. Price, a carpetbagger and Speaker of the House in 1868-69. Price was also the editor of the official party newspaper, *The Republican*, in Little Rock. In late 1868, Price opposed the excesses of militia, and Clayton immediately threatened to take away his lucrative state printing contract. The Clayton administration also threatened to impeach Price and eventually did remove him as Speaker of the House.

The *Republican's* circulation was so small that the paper could not survive without state printing business.[4] Clayton used this leverage to control the *Republican's* editorial voice, and the radicals bought most of Price's interest in the paper but kept him as editor. Price never recovered his standing with the radical politicians, even though he dropped his opposition. John McClure, the Chief Justice of the Supreme Court appointed by Clayton, received the designation as Price's advisor and editorial writer and eventually obtained an interest in the paper. This move reduced Price to a figurehead,[5] and McClure became second only to Clayton among the radicals.

More substantial opposition to Clayton came from Lieutenant Governor James M. Johnson, an Arkansas Unionist from Madison County. On April 8, 1869, Johnson and 17 other members of the General Assembly, many of them originally Unionists from northern Arkansas, signed a statement openly condemning the radical administration.[6] They especially criticized the militia excesses, the railroad subsidy, the refunding of the Holford bonds, and the administration's autocratic behavior. This declaration created a permanent breach between Clayton and Johnson.[7] However, the General Assembly had then adjourned, and Clayton had rescinded martial law in all the counties and disbanded the militia. Clayton hoped to retain enough public support to replace Alexander McDonald as U.S. Senator in 1871, so 1870 became the quietest year of the Clayton era.[8]

During the war, the Unionists in Arkansas faced considerable pressure in standing by the United States against their home state. This minority position required a great deal of courage. After the war, most Unionists were conservative and Republican, but the behavior of the radicals drove a large percentage of them back to the Democrats.

In the mid-summer of 1869, Clayton made an unannounced trip to New York. He did not notify Lieutenant Governor Johnson, and to prevent any official acts from being performed in his absence, he allegedly took the official state seal with him. The object of the trip was to sell state railroad bonds and make a few speeches telling the Northern people how well the radical government worked in Arkansas. Speeches of this nature helped seal the bonds between the Southern and Northern radicals.

During Clayton's absence, many Arkansans wanted Lieutenant Governor Johnson to seize the governor's office, call the General Assembly into session, and impeach Clayton. In a speech at Little Rock Johnson condemned the behavior of the Clayton administration but offered no hope of a coup.[9] Johnson knew that the impeachment of Clayton would fail in the State Senate, and that President Grant would furnish troops to sustain the radical governor.

Despite the lieutenant governor's resistance to a revolt, Clayton and his forces decided to remove Johnson from office. John R. Montgomery, Attorney General of Arkansas, filed a *quo warranto* proceeding against Johnson, claiming that he did not qualify for his office within the fifteen days required by the Schedule of the 1868 Constitution.[10] Clayton was elected at the same time as Johnson and did not qualify for three months. The Arkansas Supreme Court, however, in February of 1871 ruled unanimously in Johnson's favor.

Born in 1829, Johnson stumped Madison County against secession in 1861. In early 1862, he and his brother, Frank Johnson, and Isaac Murphy escaped from Madison County to the Union Army across the Missouri line. Both Johnsons served with distinction in the Union Army until the close of the War. James M. Johnson and a company of troops escorted J.R. Berry, and other Unionists, from Northwest Arkansas to Little Rock to form the Unionist Arkansas government in late 1863. He worked for Lincoln at the Republican Convention in Baltimore in 1864 and fought for the enfranchisement of the Southern people at the 1868 Republican Convention.[11] A tall, sparsely built, energetic, and independent individual, Johnson became the center of the anti-Clayton forces.

Clayton realized he had lost a lot of popular support, especially among the native Arkansas Unionists. On October 15, 1869, just after returning from New York, he received notification that he would be serenaded by his friends and would be expected to speak. In his address, Clayton admitted error, promised a fair election in November, stressed the need for lower taxes, and advocated the enfranchisement of the ex-Confederates.[12] "Let bygones be bygones; help neighbors, avoid jealousy; let us as one man and one voice strike hands together to build up the fallen fortunes of Arkansas," he said. But there were thorns in this olive branch. While conservatives wanted immediate enfranchisement by an act of the General Assembly, Clayton suggested an amendment to the 1868 Constitution, which would delay its effect until after the general election of 1872, when Grant would probably run for reelections.

These two methods of enfranchisement generated considerable

discussion for the next several months, and Clayton's method eventually prevailed. Clayton intended to win another four-year term and firmly entrench radicalism in Arkansas. The Arkansas press constantly reminded him of his promises in his famous speech of October 15, 1869, called his "October speech."

On October 14, the revolting Republicans, then called conservative Republicans, met in convention at Little Rock. Many of them had originally been Democrats but had come into the Republican Party at the time of secession, or because they felt joining the party to be the only way that they could participate in Arkansas government. General John Edwards, Alex Carloff, and H. King White were the most prominent delegates at the convention. The opposition to radicalism within the Republican Party was organized for the first time and could no longer be ignored. The platform adopted included universal suffrage, lower taxes, rights of blacks, approval of Congressional Reconstruction and the Constitution of 1868, and the formation of a new Liberal Republican Party of Arkansas.[13] This meeting of the 14th influenced Clayton to make his famous "October speech" and, since the General Assembly was not in session and the fall election of 1870 was a long way off, both sides spent their time mending fences.

Anthony A.C. Rogers of Pine Bluff, an uncompromising Unionist during the Civil War, but a friend of the Southern people after hostilities ended, represented Arkansas in Congress. He struggled in Washington for the restoration of voting rights for ex-Confederates. On March 21, 1870, Rogers spoke for removal of disabilities, reminding the representatives that many disfranchised voters were old veterans of the War of 1812, and that five years had elapsed since the Civil War had ended.[14] While Rogers was a Unionist, the people of Southeast Arkansas termed him a Democrat and willingly accepted him as their leader. On March 4, 1869, they elected him as the only Congressional Southern supporter in Arkansas.[15]

Public education began in earnest after the Civil War. The General Assembly passed the first act for public schools in 1867, which provided for a two-mill property tax to be paid only by whites. The act excluded the blacks from the schools, and provided for a State Superintendent of Public Instruction at an annual salary of $1,500. No school was to receive tax money unless it provided at least three months of schooling. Due to the 1867 Reconstruction Acts of Congress, little was done under this act except to collect $63,853.56 for the Clayton administration.[16]

In fairness, the 1868 constitution had several progressive features including Article IX which mandated the duties of the

General Assembly to provide for gratuitous education for all children between the ages of five and twenty-one years of age. The article also established a state superintendent of public education, a school tax of one dollar per capita on all male inhabitants of the state over twenty-one years of age and provided that the educational fund of the state would receive all monies both from escheat and from all unclaimed shares of estates, and certain fines. Finally, Article IX provided for the creation of a state university.

Subsequently the General Assembly passed Act 13, approved February 4, 1869, for incorporated cities and towns to form school districts. The legal voters were authorized to elect boards of directors which would have authority to conduct the grade and high schools according to certain well-defined regulations. The local boards were also charged with determining how much money was needed and the amount of taxes to levy to pay these expenses. Later the legislature passed Act 48 setting rules for the sale of school lands and the delivery of the funds to the state educational fund. These were progressive measures, but the radical actions such as the issuance of scrip prevented proper advancement in education. The governor later appointed school superintendents to serve territories to correspond to judicial districts.

On August 1, 1871, an item appeared in the *Gazette* from Monticello which illustrated the type of men often appointed as superintendents. Herbert Marr, aged 24, had been a railroad brakeman in the North before the Civil War, but remained in the South after the war. He was elected to the House in 1870, and since he served the radicals well, he was appointed district school superintendent. Since he did not know what to ask in examining a prospective teacher, he hired someone to write out both the questions and the answers. One teacher made the mistake of criticizing his grammar, and he fired her.

Marr's career in Monticello was short-lived and ended in a flurry of violence. After losing a fight with Drew County's black representative, E.A. Fulton, Marr imported John T. Murray, a black gunman from Chicago to assassinate Fulton.[17] In a separate incident, Marr's brother, Jack, wounded the son of a prominent citizen, W.T. Wells. Wells immediately avenged this shooting by killing Jack Marr.

Most school problems during Reconstruction in Arkansas tended to be financial rather than violent. In 1870, the state divided $187,427 among school districts on the basis of $1.06 per child.[18] Out of a school-age population of 180,000 in 1869, 100,000 were enrolled in schools of some nature, with an average daily attendance of 60,000. There were 2,000 teachers, of which 700 were males. The salaries of the male teachers averaged $90 per year and the females $60. The total taxes for schools, both state and district, amounted to only $577,919.44 in 1870. These were meager figures for teaching the children of an entire state with a population of 496,000, but any kind of a beginning was better than none.[19]

In spite of many educational failures, some ventures succeeded. Dr. F.M. Christian, superintendent of the 7th Judicial District embracing Pulaski, Saline, Hot Spring, Grant, Prairie, and White Counties, reported in late 1872 that the district enrollment increased from 6,667 in 1870 to 33,667 in 1871; 36 school houses were constructed in 1871 costing $9,673, and 50 houses valued at $73,691 had previously been constructed. A total of 208 teachers were employed during 1871, and the total outlay for buildings and teachers in 1871 was $41,302.[20]

But this promising start was soon ruined. The radical government issued so much script that it became worthless. The schools got scrip, not United States currency, and as a result began a five- or six-year decline. The following news story illustrates the importance of that scrip in school financing:

> The sheriffs, as tax collectors, took from the people in school taxes $184,802 in United States currency [state millage, not district]. They paid to the treasurer, Henry Page, $26,315 in currency, and the balance in state scrip, which they had purchased at about 75 cents or less on the dollar. That much wild state debt was satisfied, and the schools got the $26,315. The sheriffs [appointees of Clayton] profited by $46,200.[21]

Because of the development of the state's economy, people paid their taxes during Reconstruction. Manufacturing and diversified agriculture became increasingly important in Arkansas. Business advanced, and cotton production increased over pre-war levels and brought fair prices through 1870. But even economic growth became intertwined with the politics of the era.

The published lists of presidents and boards of directors of railroad companies nearly always included prominent radicals.

Against this background, the conservatives reorganized in 1870 even though they knew they could not defeat the radicals that year. But they did realize the importance of preventing Clayton from controlling the 1872 election.

Unquestionably, the great stumbling block to Clayton's senatorial ambition was Lieutenant Governor James M. Johnson. Both men's terms expired in January, 1873. If Clayton were elected to the Senate (U.S. Senators were then elected by the legislatures), he would have to resign as governor, and Johnson, a leading opponent, would become governor and destroy Clayton's political machine.

Clayton had to appoint the registrars by August 1, before the general election in November, and the registrars had to complete registration by September 8, or 60 days before the election. Clayton appointed his supporters as registrars, who would then register pro-Clayton voters.

The governor appointed not only the registrars but also the ten circuit judges, the ten prosecuting attorneys, a chancery judge, the Chief Justice of the Supreme Court, the commissioner of internal improvements, the solicitor general, the commissioner of state lands, ten circuit superintendents of public instruction, sixty county and probate judges, all justices of the peace and notary publics, and a multitude of other offices.[22] The appointive power of the governor practically made the state's chief executive the dictator of Arkansas. Through a governor under his control, Clayton intended to keep this power after he went to Washington as U.S. Senator, and he had no intention of losing his appointive power to Johnson.

The November 8, 1870, general election was the first after the ravages of the militia. The conservatives expected to lose most of the counties with heavy black populations but to carry the predominantly white counties. The conservatives had been diligent in registering, but when they reported to vote, as many as four or five hundred per county were told that they were not on the eligible list to vote. Their names had been scratched off the list and there was no authority to which they could appeal, except the Arkansas Supreme Court, which was also under radical control. The effects of this policy were seen in the Second Congressional District where Oliver P. Snyder, a radical, not only carried Jefferson County with a heavy black vote but also the militia-ravished, nearly white counties to the south and west. A.A.C. Rogers had been a loyal Unionist throughout the war, but that did not save him from defeat, for the radicals attacked any person not aligned with their program. It was faithfulness to radicalism, not to progress, that the radicals wanted.

The radicals won most of the seats in the General Assembly, assuring the election of a radical U.S. Senator in the up coming legislative session in January, 1871. The conservatives wanted Augustus H. Garland, but there were not enough conservative legislators to elect him. On the radical side, McDonald appeared impotent to the conservatives, and Joseph Brooks was despised for his support of the militia war and his radical viewpoints. That left Governor Clayton, for whom they had by then little respect. However, the conservatives expected his departure to the U.S. Senate to put Lieutenant Governor Johnson in the governor's chair.[23] In spite of Clayton's stranglehold, the conservatives made some small gains. The manipulation of the election was so unsavory that new efforts began immediately to prepare for the 1872 election.

The first duty of the 1871 General Assembly was to elect a U.S. Senator for a six-year term to succeed Alexander McDonald, whose term was to expire March 3, 1871. McDonald came to the South after the war and served well in the Senate, but Clayton cast him aside to get his seat.

The conservative *Gazette* on February 1 defended McDonald: Whatever may be said of his political record during the past four years, he has not been directly responsible for the crimes and infamies which will damn this present administration for all time to come. The waters of White River hid none of his victims. He has worked faithfully for the state.

McDonald made a mistake in allowing himself to be drawn under Clayton's influence. While his support got him the remainder of a U.S. Senatorial term, it destroyed his Merchants National Bank of Little Rock. The bank financed the purchase of arms thrown in the Mississippi River, and Clayton drew a draft on the bank for $11,054.45 to pay for the guns. The cashier paid the note from the school fund, but the bank was forced to reimburse the money because the school forces refused to allow their funds to pay for the sunken guns. The bank also financed legislators and convention delegates who had to wait for their money and later did not pay their notes. Both of these aids to the radicals cost McDonald money, and his bank failed.[24] McDonald soon thereafter passed out of Arkansas affairs.

In the first week of January, 1871, the General Assembly met, and Governor Clayton delivered his message to the joint houses. He congratulated the legislators on the prosperous condition of the state and the dying out of prejudice and animosities.

The assembly elected Charles Tankersley of Clark County, a radical carpetbagger, despised by the conservatives, as Speaker of the House by a vote of 51 to 21. He consistently supported the radical regime, and the press charged that Tankersley changed his name from Carswell to cover previous activities.[25] The legislature then elected Powell Clayton to the United States Senate on January 10 by a vote of 94 to 9, but the governor delayed acceptance.[26]

The House members were elected every two years, and Clayton had lost supporters there. The members of the Senate, like the governor and other state officers, were elected for four years in staggered terms, and Clayton remained supreme in that branch, for, in the beginning, his strongest men were placed there.

Senator S.W. Mallory of Pine Bluff introduced a bill in late January disqualifying from office any man who had not taken his position within the time prescribed by the constitution.[27] This act would have disqualified Johnson, and perhaps others, if rigidly enforced. The bill passed the Senate by a vote of 18 to 6 but failed to get through the House.

Voters from Pulaski and White Counties had elected Joseph Brooks to the Senate.[28] However, Brooks' election was contested, and the day after he took office the Senate voted 18 to 6 to expunge his swearing in, which effectively expelled him from the Senate.[29] To make the expulsion entirely legal, the Senate readmitted Brooks and expelled him by a vote of 16 to 7, and voted in his opponent, Wilshire Riley. This terminated the friendship between Clayton and Brooks until 1874 when they embraced each other in an unsuccessful effort to save their political careers.

On Sunday, January 29, according to press reports of the day, the radical senators held a twelve-hour conclave.[30] On the following Monday morning, January 30, the Senate Chamber resembled a military fort. All faces were tense and quiet, and police guards were all about. Those who asked about the trouble were informed that the police were there to expel Brooks, if he showed up. Johnson also had heard that if the impeachment charge passed the House, he would be subsequently tried and convicted in the Senate, and consequently did not appear.

As in Congress, impeachments in Arkansas are charged in the House, and subsequently tried in the Senate, and the effort to impeach Johnson began in the House Monday, January 30. William Hazeldine, chairman of the committee to investigate any malfeasance in office, introduced the impeachment resolution charging Johnson, the presiding officer of the Senate, with having sworn in Joseph Brooks when he had not been elected. Hazeldine quickly moved to cut off debate. Two black members, Fulton and Hawkins, denounced this "no discussion" as infamy.

Hazeldine came to Arkansas from the North about 1866 and became a teacher of black children under the dedicated Reverend Enoch K. Miller, who subsequently fired him for "moral unfitness."[31] Hazeldine subsequently rose rapidly in the radical regime and eventually became a circuit judge.

W.R. Padgett, a conservative representative from Independence and Van Buren Counties, introduced an impeachment resolution against Governor Clayton, charging him with attempting to deprive James M. Johnson of his rights to the office of lieutenant governor, with election frauds, and with taking bribes in connection with the railroad bonds. The resolution carried 42 to 36.[32] A combination of Democrats, conservative Republicans, and discontented radicals joined forces to impeach Clayton. For his part, Clayton remaind undaunted, for he knew that the Senate would find him not guilty.

Although the impeachment resolution against Johnson was first brought up and failed 38 to 39, he would have faced a 16 to 7 pro-Clayton majority in the Senate and almost certain conviction and removal. Clayton's enemies in the House were growing in number and took the initiative against him. They sent a letter to Clayton asking him if he intended to accept the position of U.S. Senator.

The opposition to Clayton in the House continued unabated. On February 17, the membership by a vote of 42 to 32 refused to receive a message from Clayton because Johnson had succeeded him while the governor was under impeachment proceedings.[33] On the same day, the impeachment of John McClure, who had been appointed Chief Justice of the state Supreme Court by Clayton, began and carried 44 to 31.[34] However, Clayton maintained his control of the Senate. To prevent the impeachment trials, 16 Clayton supporters simply failed to appear for roll call.[35] This stalemate, which went on for over a week, cost the state over a thousand dollars per day. The Senate then stood 17 for Clayton and six against, and in the House the anti-Clayton forces held an advantage of about 10 votes. Many anti-Clayton members were radicals who hated Clayton because they wanted more of the spoils. Clayton, however, had some staunch friends who organized "the invincibles" and swore to stand by him even at the risk of their lives. O.A. Hadly headed the group as captain, Attorney General J.R. Montgomery served as first lieutenant, and Conway Barbour, a black representative from Lafayette County, acted as second lieutenant.[36]

The *Gazette* suggested to Clayton's enemies that while they could not elect an anti-Clayton man to the Senate, they might defeat him with a compromise candidate, but Clayton still had the powerful weapon of patronage.[37]

On Saturday, February 24, without warning, 24 senators appeared in the Senate chamber.[38] The Clayton crowd spent the day discussing a statement attributed to anti-Clayton Senator Carloff of Benton County that the absent senators had spent their time with prostitutes. The Senate did little until March 3 when the senators notified the House that they were ready to receive the charges of impeachment against Clayton.[39] Apparently not wanting to come to trial, Clayton sent both houses a message on March 4 declining election to the Senate, and the House then tabled the impeachment charge.

Clayton had been working on an alternative plan and on March 14 he unveiled his idea.[40] Secretary of State Robert J.T. White resigned on the 13th, and Clayton appointed Johnson to fill the vacancy. The Senate immediately confirmed this appointment and Ozra A. Hadley, an unobtrusive and courteous carpetbagger senator from Little Rock, was seated as president of the Senate. This move placed Hadley in line for the governorship. Clayton was again elected to the Senate, and Hadley became a compliant caretaker of the governor's chair.

Hadley had been in Arkansas five years, and during that time had taken bankruptcy as a merchant. As a radical politician, however, he became wealthy.[41]

Almost unnoticed, on February 25, the *quo warranto* proceedings against Johnson were decided in his favor.

The chain of events resulted from Clayton's enemies and friends alike wanting to get the governor out of the state.[42] Johnson was the key to the trade, and he received vitriolic abuse, especially from the *Gazette*, and the Fayetteville *Democrat*.[43] Yet these two papers overlooked the fact that conservative leaders such as Representative J.W. House of White County aided Clayton in order to get him out of Arkansas. House later explained his vote to send Clayton to the Senate by saying:

> It was not because I approve of Clayton's administration. God forbid that I should ever approve of such a one. It was not because I loved Powell Clayton, but because I loved my country more; not because I expected to gain any favors at the hands of his excellency, but that I might be instrumental — that I might lend a helping hand for the relief of the oppressed, outraged and downtrodden people of the state of Arkansas. It was not that I expected he would do us any good in the United States Senate, but that I thought he could do us about as much harm in that body as the newsboys in the streets of New York City . . .[44]

Johnson, as lieutenant governor, had presided over a body that would have convicted him of impeachment in a moment, should the House have voted the charge, and the House had lacked only one vote in doing so. A rumor circulated that Johnson received a large farm in Madison County for agreeing to take the secretary of state appointment, but the deed records of Madison County do not support this charge. He never owned a farm of any value or ever displayed any wealth. Nor did he ever support Clayton.

Johnson served out his term as secretary of state, supporting the conservatives. The voters elected him in his own right in 1872 and he was the only state official who stood by Elisha Baxter in the so-called Brooks-Baxter War in 1874. In 1874, Johnson and Baxter were the only state officials invited to the Democratic nominating convention after the radical regime fell. Johnson was mentioned for secretary of state at the Democratic convention, but he had his name withdrawn. Johnson finished out his life in Madison County, where for 10 years he practiced medicine and served as the examiner of federal veterans for pensions.[45]

The ease with which Clayton secured a dismissal in the House of the impeachment charge shows the power of his patronage dispensation. The New York *Times* of March 19 republished an article from the Memphis *Avalanche* reporting that Clayton signed 2,000 commissions before he left. The story of this payoff has not been verified, but Clayton made a large number of political appointments.[46] The Clayton records are missing from both the office of the secretary of state and the archives of the Arkansas History Commission.[47]

After being reelected to the U.S. Senate, the former governor spoke to a crowd at the Capitol on March 14. Many in the crowd jeered him. "What about the bonds?" someone screamed. Another bellowed, "How did you get your office?" Clayton answered, "By fidelity to the Republican Party." When Clayton left for Washington on the 18th, someone ordered a band to appear at the railroad station, which facetiously played the amusing Civil War number, "Shoo Fly."[48] Before Clayton departed, he had the pleasure of seeing his friends in the Senate begin a successful movement to carve a new county out of parts of Lawrence and Sharp Counties and name it Clayton. However, the name Clayton Clunty did not last long. After the radical regime fell, the General Assembly changed the name to Clay County.

Around this time a fresh face came into prominence in Arkansas which illustrated the power of the radicals. The government created a new division of the Federal Court of the state, the Western Division, with headquarters in Fort Smith with William Story as judge. Only 28 years old and an ex-federal soldier from Oshkosh, Wisconsin, Story was a close friend of Unionist Lafayette Gregg of Fayetteville. Story had served as circuit judge in northwest Arkansas a couple of years and purchased real estate with Gregg in Fayetteville where he made his home.

This new court district comprised a large part of western Arkansas and Oklahoma as well as part of the Indian Territory. Story's position paid $6,000 per year, which was a lot for a young man whose legal training consisted of reading law in an office in Wisconsin.[49]

A second nefarious incident occurred during Hadley's administration and involved the complaints by the people who suffered theft or destruction of property by the militia in 1868. To aid these individuals, the General Assembly passed a bill April 3, 1871, providing $125,000 to those who could prove loss. Those enforcing the act were to get $5,000.

Hadley appointed the prominent radical, S.W. Mallory, as commissioner to handle the claims and gave him a year to perform the task. Those suffering loss were given six months to make their claims, and by August 1, claims of a half million dollars had been filed.[50]

Disregarding the time allowed for making claims, the commissioner paid all the money out before August 1, contrary to the Act. A.C. Cunningham, a radical attorney, received $78,868 in fees, while T.D.W. Yonley, another radical and judge, received $20,000. The Beldins and other radicals of Hot Springs were well paid, and the *Gazette* stated that they could not have lost more than the value of a chew of tobacco. Cunningham presented their claims. As far as anyone knows, the farmers and citizens who lost property never received any of the money. The incident represented blatant political stealing.

After the money was paid out, Commissioner Mallory left the state and it was several months before his name appeared again in the Arkansas press.

FOOTNOTES

[1] *Arkansas Gazette*, May 1, 1869, 2-3.
[2] *Ibid.*, January 7, 1869.
[3] *Ibid.*, January 7, 1869.
[4] *Ibid.*, March 18, 1869, 2-3.
[5] *Ibid.*, April 4, 1869, 2-1.
[6] *Ibid.*, May 14, 1869, 2-3.
[7] *Ibid.*, May 14, 1869, 2-3.
[8] *Ibid.*, July 31, 1869, 2-2.
[9] *Ibid.*, August 14, 1869, 4-1, New York *Times*, October 2, 1869, 8-1.
[10] *Ibid.*, August 18, 1869, 4-1.
[11] *Ibid.*, August 24, 1869.
[12] *Ibid.*, October 17, 1869, 4-1, and October 19, 1869, 2-2, and Fayetteville *Democrat*, October 30, 1869.
[13] *Arkansas Gazette*, October 16, 1869, 4-4.
[14] Fayetteville *Democrat*, March 28, 1870, and Pine Bluff *Weekly Press*, March 10, 1870, 2-5.
[15] *Arkansas Gazette*, August 27, 1870, 4-2.
[16] Murphy's farewell address to General Assembly and *Acts of Arkansas* 1866, p. 415.
[17] *Arkansas Gazette*, August 5, 1871, 1-2, and August 4, 1871, 2-3.
[18] *Ibid.*, June 26, 1870.
[19] *Ibid.*, December 18, 1870, 4-3.
[20] *Ibid.*, January 10, 1872, 4-3.
[21] Fayetteville *Democrat*, October 7, 1871.

[22] *Ibid.*, July 24, 1870, 2-2.
[23] Pine Bluff *Weekly Press*, November 17, 1870, 2-2.
[24] *Arkansas Gazette*, August 14, 1869, 2-1.
[25] *Ibid.*, January 21, 1871, 4-2.
[26] *Ibid.*, January 11, 1871, 2-2. New York *Times*, January 7, 1871, 1-7.
[27] *Ibid.*, January 26, 1871, 4-1.
[28] Pine Bluff *Weekly Press*, March 21, 1872, 2-3.
[29] *Arkansas Gazette*, January 26, 1871, 4-3.
[30] *Ibid.*, January 31, 1871, 2-2.
[31] Larry W. Pearce, "Enoch K. Miller and the Freemens' Schools," *Arkansas Historical Quarterly*, Vol. XXXI, No. 4, p. 325.
[32] New York *Times*, February 17, 1871, 1-4.
[33] *Arkansas Gazette*, February 18, 1871, 4-3 and 4.
[34] Fayetteville *Democrat*, February 18, 1871.
[35] *Arkansas Gazette*, February 21, 1871, 4-3.
[36] *Ibid.*, January 17, 1871.
[37] *Ibid.*, March 3, 1871.
[38] *Ibid.*, February 26, 1871.
[39] Fayetteville *Democrat*, March 4, 1871.
[40] *Arkansas Gazette*, March 14, 1871, 2-2.
[41] New York *Times*, March 19, 1871, 1-3.
[42] *Ibid.*, March 15, 1871, 1-3 and March 19, 1871, 1-3.
[43] Fayetteville *Democrat*, March 18, 1871.
[44] Harrell, p. 101.
[45] Information supplied by family and friends in Madison County.
[46] *Arkansas Gazette*, March 15, 1871, 4-4, and April 21, 1871, 2-2.
[47] Letters from the Secretary of State of Arkansas to author, July 5, 1979.
[48] *Arkansas Gazette*, March 19, 1871.
[49] *Ibid.*, April 22, 1871, 2-2, and *Southern Standard*, April 29, 1871, 2-5.
[50] *Arkansas Gazette*, August 5, 1871, 1-1.

Chapter 6

For Once, At Least, Let Us Be One

When Ozra A. Hadley succeeded Powell Clayton as governor on March 15, 1871, the entire state was tired of conflict. The citizenry wanted to evaluate the political situation, especially in relation to the general election of 1872, twenty months away.

Before the legislature adjourned March 25, a group of prominent Democrats and conservatives met to make plans to capture the state government in the next election. On March 28, the *Gazette* sounded the battle cry of those who wished to relieve the state of oppression:

In the name of God and our affected and distressed country — by all the memories of the past and hopes of the future, for once, at least, let us be one, united, indivisible in the great and momentous battle that is to come off next year.

The conservative *Gazette* continued to feed the fires of antiradicalism. On April 19-21 the paper listed the jobs that Clayton gave to 35 senators and representatives for their support and outlined how Clayton's friends used the railroad bond money to buy offices:

First, we are informed on what we believe to be good authority, that the late associate justice [Thomas M. Bowen] of the Supreme Court who was generally known as the 'Ambassador,' 'plenipotentiary,' or 'go between' for the late ex-impeached ex-governor, took $100,000 worth of bonds which had been issued to his railroad company, disposed of same for $40,000 and used the money to secure the election of the late governor to the United States Senate. Some did not want jobs and took the cash.

The gifts, small and large, were necessary to make a U.S.

Senator out of an impeached governor. The report added:

> And now for Mr. Speaker, 'the worst in the deck,' if we may be excused the expression. [Charles W. Tankersley, but his real name was Charles Carswell] He was registrar, clerk and deputy sheriff of the election in Clark County, put in four hundred and sixteen straw votes, on the names of imaginary parties who had never had a residence in the county — and elected by that means, the whole radical ticket — a senator and four representatives. He was made speaker because of his success in the frauds he practiced, and, as an additional recognition of his services, was given the position of superintendent of the penitentiary — a place where he should be making brick, instead of requiring others to do so, who were never half as bad or corrupt. His very name stinks in the nostrils of every honest man in the state.[1]

In July the *Gazette* revealed the speaker's background. Charles Carswell joined the Confederate Army early in 1861 in Virginia but deserted after about a year. He then joined the Federal Army and became a lieutenant in the 20th Pennsylvania Cavalry. The army dismissed him from that position after a trial for lying and for stealing government property. Carswell arrived in Arkansas in 1870 and Clayton sent him to Arkadelphia under the name of Charles W. Tankersley. In Clark County, he served as editor, attorney, registrar, and candidate for the lower house. Not getting enough votes, he stuffed enough false ballots (over 400) to win. Clayton subsequently arranged for him to be elected speaker.[2]

Governor Hadley was a handsome and kind man, but a weak one as well. He was the third link in Clayton's hold over the electorate, along with the ex-governor's control over the registrars, and the registrars' control over the voters. If one link failed, the dictatorship would have collapsed.

The people of Arkansas seemed willing to give Hadley a chance, but by July they knew that Chief Justice John McClure, whom Clayton left behind to direct the machine, was the boss. One of the most disliked men who came to Arkansas after the war, McClure wore a long coat and a white felt hat, used vulgar language, and enjoyed playing poker. Thomas C. Peek, a newspaperman in Arkansas political circles, accused McClure of inconsistency on some minor action and McClure denied it. Peek then facetiously agreed:

> His entire record — so far as I have any knowledge of it — is one of uniform and unbroken line of consistency stretched out upon the level plain of unvarying villainy and rascality. If he ever did a noble and virtuous act in his whole life, I have yet to hear of it.[3]

After the war, McClure started cotton farming, where good

land had been abandoned, at the Arkansas River port of Great Bend in Arkansas County, now Lincoln County. However, he lost his investment and made plans to go to La Crosse, Wisconsin. Then Congress passed the Reconstruction Acts, and recognizing the possible advantages, he stayed and prospered in radical politics.

After McClure was left in charge, he immediately became more powerful and probably more radical than Clayton. He purchased the stock of Clayton's secretary, J.H. Barton, in the *Republican*[4] and although J.C. Price kept the title of editor, McClure ran the paper and wrote most of the hard-hitting editorials.

The Fort Smith *Tri-Weekly* of March 16, 1871, carried a reprint of a sketch of McClure from the Cincinnati *Inquirer*:

John McClure, the Chief Justice of Arkansas, is a native of Putman County [Ohio]. His legal abilities were all acquired in bar rooms, at poker tables, and on the race course. He joined the Army early in the late war, and by mere exertion of 'cheek' rose to the rank of major.

At the close of the War, he squatted on a confiscated Arkansas plantation [Great Bend Plantation on Arkansas River in Arkansas County, now Lincoln County], and ingratiated himself into the good graces of the radical crew who controlled the state politically. He wrote a friend in Ohio that he could go to the U.S. Senate or become one of the supreme judges of the state, and asked his friend's advice as to which office he should accept. His friend advised the judgeship as promising more 'picking,' and McClure followed his friend's advice. He is now said to be very wealthy. Ten years ago he could have crammed all of his wealth, if reduced to greenback, in the hollow of his rotten tooth.

It is not a matter of surprise to men who know McClure that articles of impeachment have been preferred against him, but rather that he has so long escaped. He is a bold, reckless man, and would not scruple to sell his best friend, provided he could put money in his purse. No one acquainted with him would dispute his judgment in horseflesh or doubt that he would back a 'full' or a 'flush' for all they were worth, if he was the dealer; but he would be the last person to whom they would refer a case involving a principle of law.

Although the impeachment of Clayton was dropped, McClure was tried by the Senate and acquitted.

The demand for universal amnesty grew in the summer of 1871. One-third of the Arkansas voters were then disfranchised. Eventually all office holders, knowing that they could not further resist the pressure, embraced amnesty. Without amnesty, the radical hold could not have been broken for many years, and the conservative Republicans who had not yet broken completely with the radicals demanded amnesty and reform. Valentine Dell, who published the *New Era* of Fort Smith, the first Unionist paper published in the eleven seceded states, was a leading Republican who favored reform. Dell stated at a public meeting in Fort Smith in September, 1871 that the Klan, the main radical scapegoat, was non-existent and that the accusations against the Klan were made for political and partisan purposes.[5] The *Free Press* of Forrest City and The Randolph *Express*, both Republican papers, also demanded reforms. The Magnolia *Flower* (Republican) demanded the right of suffrage as soon as possible and called Clayton "the meanest and most corrupt man as ever disgraced an executive mansion." A split between radical and conservative Republicans became increasingly apparent.

The only difference between the radicals and the conservatives on giving the ballot to ex-Confederates was that the radicals who really wanted to avoid it favored the adoption of a watered-down reform and wanted to use the slower constitutional amendment process. The General Assembly could enfranchise those under disabilities at any time or in two successive sessions submit an amnesty amendment to the constitution for adoption or rejection by the voters. An amendment would delay adoption until after the 1872 election. The radicals may have anticipated that by controlling the registrars they could steal the election and defeat the amendment. They persisted in this delayed amnesty plan and it was eventually adopted in 1873.

While there was a lag in political turmoil in 1871, population growth and commercial development expanded, especially in the building of railroads. Even though the state lost many people to Texas and the Western states during the war, the population rose from 435,450 in 1860 to 483,179 in 1870,[6] an increase of 11 percent, and the assessed value of taxable property rose to $100 million in 1870.[7] Coal mining expanded in the area from Fort Smith to Clarksville, and railroads were needed to transport the coal.[8] The first thoughts of railroads in Arkansas occurred about 1850 when prominent politicians and large plantation owners began to incorporate for railroad construction. The Cairo and Fulton became the first to incorporate and was soon followed by the Memphis and Little Rock railroad.[9] By the time the Civil War began, the Memphis and Little Rock railroad had been constructed from Memphis to Madison in St. Francis County and provided the only railroad mileage in Arkansas then. Other transportation was by river boats traveling primarily on the Mississippi, Arkansas, White, and Ouachita Rivers. However, low-water periods made transportation on the Arkansas very uncertain.

The location of railroads, like the presence of navigable rivers, determined where markets and cities would develop. Everyone wanted a railroad through his community. A railroad-aid bill passed the General Assembly over Governor Isaac Murphy's veto in early 1867, but the law was never used. Under Powell Clayton's administration, interest in state aid began anew. On July 21, 1868, Clayton signed a railroad-aid bill. Many radical politicians controlled railroads as presidents or as members of their boards of directors. Railroad officials sold aid bonds without competitive bids and usually for less than par value, reaching a low of 15 percent by 1874.

Many Arkansas railroad bonds were sold in New York City. The *Journal of Commerce* in New York published a resume of Arkansas' debt in December, 1871, and the *Arkansas Gazette* reprinted the report.[10] The paper revealed that at the beginning of the war, Arkansas owed a total of $4,036,963, and when Clayton took over July 3, 1868, the debt had reached $4,829,000. By December, 1871, the general debt was $5,051,000; the railroad bonded debt $4,500,000; the levee bonded debt $1,623,000; miscellaneous floating debt of $300,000; and script over $1,000,000; for a total of $12,474,000. In three and a half years under the Clayton administration, the state's debt had risen 258 percent.

Before Clayton took over, the state's annual expenditures never exceeded $200,000, but during Clayton's tenure it increased to about $1,000,000. The state taxes were 10 mills or one per cent of the assessed valuation, county taxes averaged 20 mills, and city taxes averaged about 15 mills. The governor was one of the three members of the bond commission and had the authority to remove the other two commissioners at will. The Little Rock, Pine Bluff, New Orleans railroad made the poorest use of its bonds, completing only 18 miles of track with the $1,200,000 the company had received in bonds. "By his [Clayton's] discreditable manipulations of affairs in the state, he has overburdened the state in a debt that must, (if increased much more), result in repudiation," the *Journal of Commerce* of New York commented.

Bond fraud was common under the radicals. One example was the issuing of bonds to a Mr. Haymaker, who took them to St. Louis and hypothecated them. The Clayton aide who issued them then gave Haymaker one bond to cover the same amount. When the alleged fraud was discovered, Haymaker committed suicide. The aide said that when he issued the second papers, Haymaker promised to return the first and that he forgot to mark the second one as a duplicate.*

*This paragraph ends the report of the *Journal of Commerce* of New York.

Another example of dishonesty was the fact that the levee bonds were often not used in levee construction. They apparently were handed to the railroad officials with no guarantee of railroad or levee construction. The recipients or owners of these levee bonds were published in March, 1872, and most, if not all, were radicals. Stephen W. Dorsey, president of the Memphis to Little Rock railroad and in Arkansas only a short while, owned over $125,000 worth of these levee bonds.

Not all railroads were corrupt. The Cairo and Fulton (C. & F.) line refused the bond aid and apparently managed its affairs properly.[11] By the middle of 1871, the Little Rock to Fort Smith line was in operation from the capital city to Lewisburg (now Morrilton), the road was graded and iron ready to Clarksville, and the right-of-way was cut to Van Buren.

The radical regime interfered less with educational movements than other matters. Isaac Murphy's administration had tried to qualify an Arkansas college to receive the donation of land provided in the Morrill Act of 1862.

After the war, Congress amended the act to give the benefits to the Southern states and extended the time for acceptance until July 2, 1872. The radical government had to act fast to start a qualifying college, and the act providing for the Arkansas Industrial University, later the University of Arkansas, was signed into law March 27, 1871.[12]

The original members of the Board of Directors appointed for AIU were all either originally Unionists or carpetbaggers. The most influential one, Albert Webb Bishop, was a man of education and learning, and under his direction the school flourished. Old Main was built for only $123,885, although some of the upper floors were not completed at first. Bishop served first as treasurer of AIU and helped manage the University. Under his direction, he tried to bring Dr. A.S. Welch, president of Iowa State University, Ames, Iowa, to the institution as president. When Dr. Welch did not accept, Bishop took over the job. Then the job was offered to Confederate General Joseph E. Johnston, who refused because he said that he was not qualified. In April 1872, the school had 60 students, one of whom was black, and used an old farm building while plans were being pushed to build the building known as Old Main. By 1873, the school had 230 students although most of those did only preparatory work.[13]

Along with education, agriculture revived after the war. By 1872, Arkansas raised more cotton than before the war, and the state actually led the South in cotton production that year.[14] Cities grew rapidly, especially Little Rock, which expanded from 3,000 people in 1860 to 15,000 by 1870. The war aided the growth of the capital city by attracting people looking for protection from the chaos generated by the violence in the hinterland.

During the Hadley administration, violence continued. Arkansas witnessed the Pope County war, the Chicot County war, the Crittenden County war, and several other minor outbreaks. The Pope County war between Confederates and non-Confederates began over a trivial matter. One day, the radical deputy sheriff, John Williams, came into Dover, the old county seat of Pope County, with a bullet hole in his hat and in his sleeve. His brother, Sheriff W. Morris Williams, was a Unionist who had been murdered in 1866.[15] The shooting of John Williams consequently touched off a round of revenge murders on both sides. The Pope County war showed that the Hadley administration lacked the capability of handling conflict.

The Crittenden County war was a carryover of murders that occurred during the earlier militia war. In the later struggle, a young man named Clarence Collier, who sympathized with the local people against the radicals, deliberately shot and killed the county clerk, a Mr. Haynes. Haynes had befriended several blacks and the blacks searched out Collier and killed him in retaliation for the Haynes murder.

In Chicot County, the black population was four times as great as the white population, and consequently the voters elected only black officials. James Mason, a mulatto, served as the leader of the black community. Before the war, his white father sent him North and to Europe for an education. The radicals at first offered Mason the position of minister to the black Republic of Liberia in Africa, which had been settled by free blacks from America.[16] Mason declined this position, and the voters elected him to the State Senate in 1868. In the first election for the U.S. Senate in the General Assembly in 1871, Mason voted for Governor Powell Clayton.[17]

Clayton then appointed Mason as Chicot County Judge, but the Senate did not approve the appointment. Clayton then appointed as judge a Mr. Ragland, and another carpetbagger, Conway Barbour, a black representative from Lafayette County, as Chicot County assessor and registrar.[18] Barbour had never been in Chicot County before his appointment, which aroused considerable resentment in the County. On the next ballot for senator Mason voted for J.T. White, an outstanding black from Helena. Mason assumed the position of county judge even though he had not been confirmed, and he controlled the county for several years. He feuded with Ragland and Barbour during much of that time.

In a contest for the election of delegates to the Republican state convention, one of Barbour's followers was killed in 1872. Another black man, F.D. Walker, became sheriff and contended for control of the county with Mason, who finally shot Walker in the arm.[19] Ragland and other opponents finally left Mason in control.

Further elements that led to the Chicot County war included a controversey over a railroad promoted by the radicals, the Mississippi, Ouachita, and Red. The railroad was to run from Eunice on the Mississippi River in northern Chicot County to about 160 miles west to the Texas border. Over a million dollars in bonds had been provided for this project, but the money was soon squandered with only a few miles of track built. The promoters began asking the counties that the railroad was to pass through to vote additional money for the project. A vote for $250,000 was scheduled for Chicot County. The white minority owned most of the land, paid most of the taxes and understandably opposed the expenditure. The blacks paid few taxes and fell under the radical influence to support the proposition.[20]

A black lawyer from Washington named Wynn got into a heated argument about the railroad in a Lake Village store with a white man, John H. Sanders. In the ensuing struggle, Wynn knocked Sanders to the floor. Curtis Garrett, the store owner, gave Sanders a knife, and he killed Wynn.[21] Another white man named Dugan was present and advised the men, for their safety, not to leave the store. The three white men were arrested and jailed by Mason on December 12, 1871.[22] Two days later a black mob took the three men from the jail and lynched them.[23] One account reported Garrett had fifty bullet holes in his body and all three bodies were mutilated.[24] The mob then ransacked the store, robbed the families of the lynched men of their cash, killed livestock, and ran off the white people who had not already fled. The mob filled the vacant houses with bullet holes. Mason's power here should have enabled him to prevent this affair, but he blamed it on the Ku Klux Klan even though it was nonexistent there. Some conservative press reports said Mason and the prosecuting attorney, Derry Downs, led the mob.[25]

Governor Hadley organized fourteen state militiamen and sent them by boat to Chicot County. When they returned, with one man's hair pulled out, they reported "everything now quiet."[26]

During the next term of the circuit court, Judge H.P. Morse, appointed by Governor Clayton in 1868, decried the loss of Mr. Wynn, speaking well of him. In a different manner and without mentioning names, he spoke of the ones who were lynched as "the killers."

By August 1871, opponents of the Clayton-McClure-Hadley

government had launched a counter-offensive against the radicals. On August 21 the conservatives held one of their first meetings in White County. J.N. Cypert remarked: "Thieves to the rear; honest men for office," which became the conservatives' battle cry through the 1872 general election. The Northern opponents of Grant had actually first adopted this slogan.[27]

Another source of opposition came from Joseph Brooks. Brooks, as a member of the Arkansas House of Representatives in 1868, had tried to make himself the champion of Clayton's brutal militia policy, but Clayton never accepted Brooks and thwarted virtually all his attempts for office. Brooks began to oppose Clayton after the governor kept him from being elected to the U.S. Senate in 1868. That December, Brooks criticized the General Assembly for its unnecessary expenses,[28] and by 1871, the break between the two men became public. In a speech at Monticello in August, Brooks accused Clayton of thievery and other crimes and then delivered several other similar speeches.[29] Brooks appointed himself as the leader of the opposition, and the Democrats had to choose between joining Brooks or opposing the divided Republican Party.

As the Republican division widened, a special correspondent of the Indianapolis *Sentinel*, who signed his article "Americus," interviewed Governor Hadley. After the interview began, McClure entered the room uninvited, and the governor stopped talking and referred the correspondent to McClure, who then answered all questions.[30]

Powell Clayton was a friend of Grant and readily affiliated his radical faction of the Republican Party in Arkansas with him. Grant had been their protector in the South with troops, or with the threat of troops. Radicals everywhere in the South struggled for Grant's re-election. The resurging Southern conservatives had to decide if they would field their own slate or join the revolting Republicans.

It remained for a German-American, Carl Schurz, who reached the United States in 1852, to point to proper non-partisan reconstruction. On July 22, 1872 at the St. Louis conservative convention, he stated in polished English:

> The first great object of our policy [Republican administration of Grant] should have been to renationalize the South; to revive among the Southern people feelings calculated to attach their hearts again to the fortunes of the union. For, let us not indulge in the delusion that the holding together by force of its component parts can long endure. It requires that bond which binds together the hearts of the people, and not their borders

only; and to create that bond which was for us the highest object of statesmanship.[31]

This division in the Arkansas Republican ranks had been brewing for years dating back to the James M. Johnson revolt and included other defections from the Clayton faction. On October 15, 1869, when Governor Clayton made a speech trying to placate the Southern people, he offered them eventual amnesty. Robert F. Catterson, a leading militia general, reprimanded him for his promise and called the governor a liar. Clayton, who had only one hand, slapped him. Catterson replied that he would no sooner hit a one-handed man that he would a woman.

Colonel W.G. Whipple, another radical, joined Catterson in criticizing Clayton. Catterson and Whipple were the marshal and the district attorney, respectively, for the Federal Court of the Eastern District of Arkansas, and as soon as Clayton reached Washington, they had him indicted by a federal grand jury on the charge that he falsely certified John Edwards as the elected Representative instead of Thomas Boles. Both men, as well as Joseph Brooks, federal tax collector, and J.L. Hodges, Little Rock postmaster, then lost their jobs.[32] Isaac C. Mills and S.R. Harrington, Clayton's friends, replaced Catterson and Whipple. The following year, Colonel Logan H. Root was dismissed as marshal of the Western District Court of Arkansas for supporting the Greeley-Brown ticket for president against Grant. One characteristic of the radicals, both state and national, was their ruthlessness in dismissing any man who did not follow party regularity.

In 1871-72 Clayton spent his time in Washington making accusations against the Arkansas Ku Klux Klan. The Klan was never strong in Arkansas and played only a small part in politics, primarily in the poor, predominately white rural sections. Clayton said that the Klan "numbered not in hundreds, but in hundreds of thousands — 30,000 in Arkansas . . . it was military in character." He called the Ku Klux Klan "the second revolt," and claimed it to be almost as powerful as the first. He emphasized that he fought the Klan with his militia.[33]

Clayton depicted the Klan as marching in bands over the state whipping blacks and Unionists and cheating the nation of the fruits of the victory.

On May 2, 1871, General Sherman responded at New Orleans to Clayton's remarks about the Ku Klux Klan:
> I probaby have as good means of information as most persons in regard to what is called the Ku Klux Klan, and am perfectly satisfied that the thing is greatly over-estimated; and if the Ku Klux bills were kept out of Congress and the Army kept at

their legitimate duties, there are enough good and true men in all Southern states to put down all the Ku Klux or other bands of marauders.[34]

Joseph Brooks, after making it known that he no longer supported Clayton, spent his time making himself the leader of the anti-Clayton forces in Arkansas. He challenged Clayton to meet him, but Clayton refused. Ozra Hadley had been such a failure in keeping peace in Pope, Crittenden, and Chicot Counties that neither Republican faction considered him for the ticket in 1872.

The last few months of 1871 and the first two of 1872 were fairly quiet in Arkansas. In 1871, Joseph Brooks made a number of speeches in the larger towns attacking Clayton but did not claim to be a candidate for office. The real fight was to come in 1872, a presidential election year. Horace Greeley likewise was speaking in the larger cities of America attacking Grant. Brooks and Greeley both asked for complete amnesty and enfranchisement of ex-Confederates.

Brooks and Clayton made only a few speeches in the last half of 1871, and they usually attacked each other. At a Grant Club meeting in Little Rock September 26, Clayton attacked the Klan, the rebels, and Brooks, but Clayton's remarks turned the meeting into bedlam because Brooks attended with several of his own followers. The riotous meeting foreshadowed what was to come.

FOOTNOTES

[1] *Arkansas Gazette*, April 21, 1871.
[2] *Ibid.*, July 6, 1871, 2-2.
[3] *Ibid.*, May 1, 1871.
[4] *Ibid.*, May 23, 1871, 2-2.
[5] Fort Smith *Weekly Herald*, September 5, 1871.
[6] *Tri-Weekly*, May 13, 1871.
[7] Pine Bluff *Daily Appeal*, March 15, 1871, 1-1.
[8] *Arkansas Gazette*, August 15, 1871.
[9] *Ibid.*
[10] *Ibid.*, December 28, 1871, 1-1.
[11] The C & F began by act of Congress February 9, 1853 and was reaffirmed July 28, 1866. Under the first act, this road was given every alternate section of land on each side of the road and back for five sections. The second act gave it land for ten sections back. This was the standard amount given for railroad construction all over the United States. See Ark. Statutes 1947 Annotated, p. 307.
[12] Fayetteville *Democrat*, November 6, 1875.
[13] *Ibid.*, November 29, 1872.
[14] *Arkansas Gazette*, November 26, 1872, 2-2.
[15] Letter February 3, 1975, to author from Beatrice V. Worsley, New Cuyama, California, grand-niece of the two Williams men.
[16] *Arkansas Gazette*, May 11, 1871, 2-2.

[17] *Ibid.*
[18] Ibid., April 17, 1871, 2-2.
[19] *Ibid.*, May 9, 1871, 2-3.
[20] *Ibid.*, December 21, 1871, 1-2.
[21] Pine Bluff *Weekly*, May 23, 1871, 2-4.
[22] *Democrat*, December 30, 1871.
[23] Pine Bluff *Weekly Press*, February 8, 1872, 2-2.
[24] New York *Times*, December 29, 1871, 2-4.
[25] *Arkansas Gazette*, November 7, 1872. 2-3, and New York *Times*, December 29, 1871, 2-4.
[26] New York *Times*, December 27, 1871, 2-4, and Arkadelphia *Southern Standard*, January 6, 1872, 2-5.
[27] *Arkansas Gazette*, September 21, 1871, 1-2.
[28] *Ibid.*, December 4, 1868, 2-1.
[29] *Ibid.*, August 15, 1871, 1-1.
[30] *Ibid.*, August 23, 1871, 1-1.
[31] Fort Smith *Weekly Herald*, August 3, 1872, 2-2.
[32] *Arkansas Gazette*, June 28, 1871, 2-2.
[33] *Ibid.*, April 21, 1871, 1-1, and April 27, 1871, 2-2.
[34] *Ibid*, May 9, 1971, 1-3.

Chapter 7

To Be Governor Or Die Trying

By March, 1872, the revolting Republicans had not nominated any candidates for state office. Instead, Joseph Brooks had nominated himself. He knew exactly what he wanted; he wanted to be governor. Previously, he had been stymied by the Clayton division of the Republican Party in every move, and he was determined to defeat his opponent by going directly to the people rather than to packed radical conventions. He had been campaigning for a year by advertising his speaking dates all over the state, and whenever he could find an audience, he spoke two to three hours at a time.

Brooks was a person of considerable personaltiy, ability, and education. Born in 1821 either in Cincinnati, or just across the Ohio River in Kentucky, Brooks entered the ministry in the Ohio Conference of the Methodist Church at the age of nineteen, transferred to Iowa in the early forties, and held a pastorship at Fairfield, Iowa, in 1847. He was elected in 1856 editor of the *Christian Central Advocate* by the General Conference and was associated with Northwestern University from 1854 to 1858, serving on the Board of Directors from 1855 to 1858. He successfully sold scholarships in Iowa for Northwestern during several of these years.[1]

At the outbreak of the Civil War, Brooks entered the Federal Army as a chaplain. Immediately after the war, he became active in politics in Arkansas. He gained prominence in the Constitutional Convention of 1868, especially because of his advocacy of the freedman's rights.

In December of 1871, Brooks went to Washington to help Thomas Boles, a rebel Republican in his contest with John J. Edwards, a Clayton Republican, for the Third District seat in North and West Arkansas as Representative in Congress. He succeeded and returned to Arkansas around March 1, 1872.[2] Losing no time in launching his candidacy for governor, Brooks fired his first shot at city hall in Little Rock on the evening of March 4, speaking for two hours. He had generated a large crowd (half blacks, half whites) with circulated hand bills, and from that moment on Brooks became a candidate for governor.[3]

During his stay in Washington, Brooks probably heard some of the speeches of Senator Carl Schurz, considered by many as the greatest speaker of his day. Although Brooks neither quoted Schurz directly nor gave him credit, he often used words similar to those used by the Senator. Brooks used Biblical remarks as he had always done: "The Sabbath was made for man, not man for the Sabbath." Likewise, he said, "the party is made for man, not man for the party," a statement Schurz had made before. Thus Brooks justified his abandonment of the radical Republican Party, not the principles of republicanism or the Republican name. Being a minister, Brooks gave a religious tone to his speeches, "Freedom, liberty, and equality before the law came down to us through the generations from God himself." Brooks condemned the thieves and indicated Powell Clayton was the chief one. In his March 4 speech, he hurled a challenge to Clayton and Hadley: "Count us out and be damned."

The Arkansas situation paralleled that of the nation. The national meeting of those revolting against Grant was held at Cincinnati May 1. Those Republicans, too, were an inexperienced group, and they nominated Horace Greeley, editor of the New York *Daily Tribune*, for President, and B. Gratz Brown, governor of Missouri, for Vice President.

The New York *Times* in an editorial of June 24, commented that Democrats had more animosity for Greeley than any man except Wendell Phillips, and his nomination distressed Schurz. In addition to the many slogans and campaign cries, the Greeley group in the North and the Brooks followers in Arkansas spoke of their movement as the "New Departure," a term first used by the copperhead, Clement L. Vallandigham of Ohio.[4]

The Grant Republicans immediately attacked Greeley for his sarcastic remarks about the Democrat Party during his anti-slavery days. Perhaps Greeley's bitterest reproach of the campaign was the caricature drawings of him by political cartoonist Thomas Nast, depicting him as a man of low intelligence.[5]

Brooks, though not yet nominated by any group, began his campaign at Washington, Arkansas on May 4, speaking against Senator Clayton and in favor of honesty in office, amnesty for all citizens, and for "thieves to the rear; honest men for office." His speeches were loud, long, and forceful, and in the end, he used the melodramatic words of the British war poet, Thomas Campbell (1777-1844):

The combat deepens. On ye brave,
Who rush to glory, or the grave.[6]

Brooks drew large crowds wherever he spoke. The Fort Smith *Herald* reported that 3,000 to 5,000 people cheered him at Ozark. For that speech 600 people were ferried across the Arkansas River from the south half of Franklin County to hear this phenomenal speaker.[7]

Brooks and other rebellious members of the Republican Party met in Little Rock on May 20. The group adopted an admirable platform, as most conventions do, and officially nominated Brooks for governor and a full slate of candidates for state offices. Brooks spoke to the convention from the State House steps on the 21st and stumped the state until election day in November.

The Arkansas supporters of Brooks called themselves the Greeley-Brown ticket, although the candidate's fiery oratory did not appeal to all the conservative leaders. He was quoted as having said he would be elected governor or die trying. The *Gazette* suggested for governor Augustus H. Garland, Isaac Murphy, or Dr. John Kirkwood and that the candidate run on a fushion ticket of both conservative Republicans and Southern Democrats. Brooks limited his ticket to conservative Republicans.

The *Gazette* agreed with the Washington *Telegraph* that any of these three men, if supported by conservative Republicans, would be hard to beat. The paper also felt that Brooks would be difficult to defeat in a congressional race. However, the Little Rock *Journal* (a short-lived partisan paper) replied for Brooks that he would run only for governor and would remain a Republican The *Journal* intimated, however, that if two candidates ran against the Clayton machine, both would be defeated, and that if the Democrats put a candidate in the field, Brooks would withdraw.

Although Brooks had become a staunch opponent of radicalism, many Southern Democrats remembered Brooks' radical behavior in the Constitutional Convention of 1868 and his support of Clayton's murderous militia attacks. Other Southerners, however, soon began to feel that Brooks had truly changed in the last year, and the ex-Confederates rapidly lined up with Brooks. To get the ex-Confederates' support. Brooks promised he would fill the penitentiary so full of radical thieves that their arms and legs would stick out the door and windows. Although Brooks' enemies feared him, many conservatives still did not trust him. They especially remembered his waste-howling wilderness speech in which he defended Clayton's militia attacks.[8]

The Democratic state convention met on June 19, and it was one of the largest ever held in Arkansas.[9] The roster contained the strongest pre-war conservatives of the Democratic and Whig Parties of Arkansas, including General Fagan, M.L. Bell, Fay Hempstead, R.C. Newton, A.A.C. Rogers, Ben T. Duvall, and Harris Flanigan. However, the convention refused to place a candidate on Brooks' ticket. Brooks spoke for an hour or more on the steps of the Capitol, in an effort to get the Democrats' endorsement. During the speech, he outlined a platform of lower taxes, full amnesty for disfranchised voters, and court reform.

Many listeners on the Capitol steps were skeptical and one heckler asked Brooks to explain his "howling wilderness" speech. He explained that he meant it was the duty of the state government to make the state peaceable and law abiding, or a howling wilderness would prevail from the Missouri border to the Red River. His explanation convinced enough listeners to draw cheers. Castigating every branch of the radical state government, including the state courts, Brooks stated that "With rare exceptions, the judicial ermine is dragged in the filth."

The convention nominated presidential electors who supported Greeley and Brown but did not nominate a ticket for governor or other state offices. A few days later the national Democratic Party endorsed Greeley and Brown, who had already been nominated by the rebelling Republicans of the North. Brooks felt reassured by the Democratic support and set off on another swing around the state. His campaign committee included ex-Confederate and Democratic leaders such as Gordon N. Peay, Fay Hempstead, and Harris Flanigan.[10]

This campaign had been going on for a year or more, and until the radicals held their convention in August it was just routine hard speaking by Brooks, and his speeches were all similar. Brooks made four to six speeches per week in towns twenty to forty miles apart, presumably traveling by buggy over terrible roads. Many progressives and intellectuals who were determined to have a good government supported him.

Brooks' primary strength in this campaign centered on his anti-Clayton stand, because had done little else to endear himself to the people of Arkansas.

FOOTNOTES

1. Letter to author from Northwestern University Archives, August 14, 1974.
2. *Arkansas Gazette*, March 3, 1872, 4-3.
3. *Ibid.*, March 6, 1872, 1-1.
4. *Ibid.*, October 2, 1872, 2-5.
5. Basset, p. 649.
6. *Arkansas Gazette*, May 16, 1872. 1-1.
7. Fort Smith *Tri-Weekly*, August 10, 1872.
8. Fort Smith *Tri-Weekly Herald*, January 20, 1872.
9. *Southern Standard*, June 29, 1872, 1-4.
10. New York *Times*, June 19, 1872, 1-3, and June 24, 1872, 1-2.

Chapter 8

The Echo of Powell Clayton

On August 20, the long-awaited 1872 Republican State Convention under the control of the Grant-Clayton faction assembled at Little Rock. Ozra Hadley realized he could not receive the gubernatorial nomination and many feared that a radical could not win even with their control over the registrars. Therefore, on the 21st, the convention nominated the genteel, honest, and relatively unknown Arkansas Unionist, Judge Elisha Baxter of Batesville.[1]

In the Poland investigation two years later, Baxter related that Clayton mentioned to him several months before the convention that he [Baxter] might be the nominee for governor. Clayton wanted to secure the votes of many Democrats who remembered that Brooks had once been their enemy and that Baxter was an Arkansas Unionist, not a Northern carpetbagger. Clayton assumed he could control the genteel Baxter as he had Hadley,[2] but the ex-governor overlooked Baxter's honesty and courage.

Had Clayton observed Baxter's behavior closely, he would have seen that he would be no stooge. In September, 1871, Baxter had issued a writ of mandamus requiring a sheriff to hand over school taxes collected for the school authorities. As late as February, 1872, Hadley had appointed a sheriff of Lawrence County in opposition to a five-to-one majority of the quorum court. Judge Baxter refused to accept the sheriff's bond, which was signed by Little Rock radicals when Lawrence County people refused to sign. Baxter then accepted the sheriff designated by the quorum court of Lawrence County. This action typified Baxter's decisiveness. He was a gentle and honorable person in an age of murder, thievery, and rascality. But since he had not spoken out against debaucheries elsewhere, no one realized he was a man of strength and determination.

Baxter may not have known the full extent of the debauchery in the Clayton machine, but he knew of the cruelties of D.P. Upham and his militia at Augusta. He also knew of the charge that Brooks received $25,000 for pushing the bill to refund the questionable Holford Bonds of the Arkansas Real Estate Bank through the 1868 General Assembly. Independence County, Baxter's home, was predominantly white with a lot of independent and pre-war Unionist sentiment, and Baxter had actually been imprisoned by the Confederates, which influenced him to join the Republican Party. He may have felt that if he did not accept this nomination, it might go to one who would oppress the people of Arkansas. This reasoning is further supported by Baxter's statement to the Democratic convention in 1874 that he was given an honorable platform and in carrying it out, he violated no trust.

In accepting the nomination, Baxter spoke kindly of the blacks who comprised half of the convention and had helped him during his prison term. His was a peace-making speech toward almost everyone except Joseph Brooks, although he did not attack him seriously. He said the word "carpetbagger" had almost never passed his lips. He endorsed the Grant-Wilson national presidential ticket and spoke well of Clayton and Hadley, as everyone expected him to do.[3]

Never a loud or aggressive speaker, Baxter meant what he said. The German-born editor and educator, Valentine Dell of Fort Smith, initially complimented Baxter, but after hearing his acceptance speech, said Baxter was weak and would become Clayton's tool.[4] Another radical who heard him reportedly said, "He is just silly enough to be honest."

Volney Voltaire Smith, a radical in the Clayton-McClure camp, received the nomination for lieutenant governor. Smith had been only a clerk of Lafayette County and few people knew anything about him. He was a nonentity, everyone believed, selected to take Baxter's place as a stooge if Baxter proved not to be one. Stephen Wheeler was nominated for auditor against incumbent James R. Berry, and J.C. Corbin, a black graduate of Oberlin and a carpetbagger, was nominated for Superintendent of Public Instruction against Dr. Thomas Smith, a white carpetbagger incumbent.[5]

Baxter began his campaign by rejecting Brooks's invitation to debate, claiming that Brooks had not been nominated by any party. The Judge's speech at his home town of Batesville on August 27 was weak, dull, and poorly received. He said he was glad Powell Clayton and Ozra Hadley were his friends and referred again to the charge that Brooks had accepted $25,000 for his part in pushing the bill to refund the disputed Holford Bonds through the 1868 General Assembly. Later Baxter and Clayton traveled and spoke together, and Clayton gradually took over the heavy speaking, even though he was not a candidate, indicating he was carrying Baxter while speaking for Grant.

In a letter to Dr. Weldon E. Wright in October, 1872, Baxter showed his intentions during the campaign:

If the people of Arkansas do me the honor to elect me to the office of Governor of the state, I shall only be willing to accept that position for the express purpose of being the governor of and for the whole people of the state, and shall never condescend to be the governor of any party, clique, or ring merely. .. I mean to devote my whole time to the services of what I consider to be the best interests of the whole people of the state.[6]

Of course, this letter represents standard principles that practically all politicians have always claimed.

The most commonly held view of Baxter was expressed by a journalist who signed his name "High Private." After half a column of abusing Baxter and predicting eight more years of radical thieving, he wrote:

Did I ever tell you about my first meeting with Baxter and my impression on that occasion? It was in the Mountain Hotel in Fayetteville on the night of the 28th of September last. On that day Clayton and Baxter had spoken at Cane Hill, and, as usual, had been eudgeled [sic] and belabored with merciless severity by Old Brindle [Brooks] and Hynes. In the evening, like whipped dogs, they slunk away for Fayetteville to prepare for another skinning on the morrow. They drove up to the hotel about nine o'clock at night and alighted. They came into the office in the following order: Clayton first, with that quick nervous step which characterized that artful schemer. Baxter next with that awkward ungainly carriage which marks the so called . . . After entering the house Clayton walked to the desk and registered — Baxter stood with a satchel in one hand, and the other hand in his pocket, saying nothing and looking like a poor boy at a frolick . . .

'Suppose we retire,' said Clayton.

'Certainly,' said Baxter.

They went, Clayton with the quick feline movement and, Baxter with the awkward, ungainly step . . . I soliloquized to myself: If that awkward and evidently weak man should be governor, he would be but the echo of Powell Clayton. Baxter will be the throne, Clayton the power behind the throne. I did not seek an interview on that night, because it was my business to watch and draw conclusions — then again they were distinguished minstrel officials, and I only High Private[7]

High Private was not the only journalist who thought that Baxter would be a stooge.[8] Soon after Baxter's nomination, the Pine Bluff *Press* insinuated that he had been a slave holder and would be the shadow of Powell Clayton. The ex-Confederates fell in behind Brooks, not because they admired him, but because he had fallen out with Clayton, their hated enemy.

The intensity of the campaign was illustrated by a confrontation that became a legend in Arkansas politics.

William J. Hynes was a conservative at-large candidate for Congress against John M. Bradley. During the campaign, Hynes and Brooks met the Clayton-Baxter party at Oliver Springs in Crawford County. Hynes accused Clayton of wearing a secessionist cockade in Kansas in 1861. Clayton yelled, "You are a liar." And Hynes replied, "You are a liar and a thief."[9]

Stories differ about what happened next. Clayton claimed that he ran after Hynes, who fled. The conservative *Gazette*, however, on September 10 claimed Clayton had a pistol when he chased Hynes. In the end both called the other a liar and a thief. The story received wide publicity and only served to disgust Arkansas people with both politicians. John M. Harrell indicated that Baxter smiled at this incident and made his normal speech, indicating that Baxter was beginning to understand Clayton and was doing what he thought best.

Baxter often affirmed his belief that Brooks was dishonest. In his acceptance speech at the Republican Convention on August 21, he made a statement which he repeated during the campaign.

> The cry of this eminent man [Brooks] 'Honest men to office.' I should not like to see any man occupy any office. however small, unless he is a hundred times more honest than I believe the Reverend Joseph Brooks to be.[10]

Apparently the Arkansas conservatives became disgusted with the accusations of both sides and finally nominated the popular Reverend Andrew Hunter as a Democratic candidate for governor. The *Gazette*, which had given Brooks a lukewarm endorsement, joined the Hunter movement.[11] Hunter, however, soon withdrew, and his supporters, including the *Gazette*, half-heartedly returned to the Brooks camp.[12] Some observers believed the Hunter movement was secretly prompted by the Clayton faction in order to split Brooks's support.

The November 5 election was marked by charges and countercharges of fraud, and each side claimed they had won the election.

A close examination of the returns shows that many all-white counties were controlled by Brooks and were just as solidly for him as other counties with heavy black populations were strong for Baxter.[13] This indicates that the ex-Confederates and conservatives supported Brooks, and the blacks, radicals, and some conservatives voted for the Baxter ticket. The dominant party faction in each county turned in a lopsided vote count for their ticket. An example of the one-sided results reported was the tally in Saline County of 900 to 9 for Brooks.

A favorite radical trick was to listen for complaints of fraud in counties favorable to Brooks and throw out the votes of that county. Governor Hadley and his registrars managed to do this in several counties to Baxter's advantage.

The 1868 Constitution required that in case of a contested election for state officials the question would be decided by a joint vote of both houses of the General Assembly.[14] The Brooks forces knew that Powell Clayton controlled the General Assembly, and there was talk of a citizens' establishment of Brooks as governor.[15] Brooks, however, declined to take this dangerous step because he probably believed he would win by legal means.[16] However, at a conservative gathering in Little Rock on November 18 he said he was elected by 15,000 votes, and "A man elected should take and hold office." Because of the type campaign the two men ran, Brooks's unpopularity and Baxter's popularity both developed rapidly after the election. Conservatives were gradually swinging to Baxter.

Brooks supporters held a convention in Little Rock on January 4, but only twelve counties sent representatives. The delegates discussed the forcible takeover of the governor's office but they realized that Brooks's support was ebbing, evidenced by the fact that few Democrats attended the meeting.

The General Assembly met Monday, January 6, 1873, and the radicals had 19 senators and 52 representatives, and the conservatives had 5 senators and 24 representatives. They declared Baxter the winner in the election by a popular vote of 41,684 to 38,726, and John McClure, Chief Justice, swore him in as the new governor. However, the above tabulation was based upon the returns which had come in. No explanation has ever been made about why four counties and many districts never sent in their results, or why Brooks made no effort to get them in.

The 1872 election was the last one held in Arkansas in which the ex-Confederates were disfranchised, and the last one won by the radicals. The election launched one of the strangest and most important gubernatorial administrations in the history of the ten Southern states subject to Congressional Reconstruction. During the course of that administration it was a course of action hatched and executed in the lonely, unobtrusive, unassisted (at first), and stubborn but honest and unselfish mind of Elisha Baxter. Elisha Baxter completely dismantled the Powell Clayton machine, much to everyone's surprise.

The Greeley-Brown ticket for president also lost. At the time of his presidential campaign, Greeley and his wife were both ill. Grant received 3,597,070 votes and Greeley 2,830,403. The disfranchised Southern vote, mostly Greeley's, could have wiped out much of that difference. Greeley's wife died at the time of the election and he also expired a month later.

Grant's re-election surely pleased Clayton, perhaps making him feel that the Republican Party was secure in national politics. In the Arkansas campaign he gave a lot of time and energy, spent a lot of money, and applied a lot of pressure to his followers. He probably felt that in the following four years he would seal his control of Arkansas for much of the nineteenth century.

The re-election of Grant also discouraged Brooks from trying to take the governorship by force, because the President used federal troops in several states to keep radicals in office. Brooks, having tied his campaign to Greeley's national ticket, had little opportunity to ask for a congressional investigation. Thus whatever inquiry would be made by him would have to wait until he could get the matter into Arkansas courts and there seemed to be no popular demand for either a court or a congressional investigation.

FOOTNOTES

[1] New York *Times*, August 22, 1872, 5-5.
[2] *Ibid.*, August 22, 1872, 5-5, and August 23, 1872, 1-4.
[3] *Arkansas Gazette*, August 22, 1872, 4-3.
[4] Fort Smith *Weekly Herald*, August 31, 1871.
[5] New York *Times*, August 23, 1872, 1-3.
[6] *Arkansas Gazette*, May 23, 1873, 2-2.
[7] Fort Smith *Tri-Weekly Herald*, February 8, 1973, 1-1.
[8] Van Buren *Press*, September 19, 1872, 2-4.
[9] *Arkansas Gazette*, September 10, 1872.
[10] Harrell, p. 139.
[11] New York *Times*, October 2, 1872, 1-7.
[12] *Arkansas Gazette*, October 29, 1872, 2-5.
[13] *Ibid.*, November 19, 1872, 4-6.
[14] New York *Times*, October 30, 1872, 1-1.
[15] *Arkansas Gazette*, November 19, 1872, 4-4.
[16] New York *Times*, January 7, 1873, 1-7.

Chapter 9

Who Was Elisha Baxter?

Elisha Baxter was one of the greatest and yet most unrecognized statesmen in Arkansas. He was born near Rutherford, North Carolina, on September 1, 1827, and received a limited common school education. He apparently attended Princeton Academy at Owensboro, Kentucky, and the town paper in later years proudly announced that his name was chiseled on a campus tree.[1] His older brother, John Baxter, became a respected U.S. Circuit Judge in Tennessee. Their father was an Irish immigrant.[2]

Elisha and his younger brother, Taylor Baxter, with their families, moved to Batesville, Arkansas, in 1853 and bought a store. This venture failed, and by 1855 the brothers were virtually penniless. They acted honorably, however, surrendering all their property, including their homes and slaves. Elisha had been studying law and received his license to practice about the time the store went under, which eventually enabled him to pay all of the store debts.[3]

Baxter was elected in the Arkansas House of Representatives from Independence County in 1854 as a Whig. The Whig Party was dying, and his name does not appear in the following 1856 General Assembly. Apparently wanting to affiliate with a party, Baxter took part in the Democratic Congressional nominating convention of 1856, serving as secretary. He was elected to the House again in 1858 as a Democrat. Even though he was not a secessionist, he was elected prosecuting attorney as a Democrat in 1860. He took the customary Confederate office holders' oath and served as prosecuting attorney until about the time the Federal troops marched westward through Independence County in 1862.

Lacking the desire to fight the United States, Baxter remained in Batesville rather than to flee west to Little Rock. This brought him substantial criticism, and when the Federals retreated back toward the Mississippi River, he fled north. By this time Baxter had been offered a commission by the Federals, but he refused to take arms against either side. Some authorities said General Thomas C. Hindman, who had been made a virtual military dictator of Arkansas in 1862, issued a "living or dead" order for him, on the basis that Baxter had violated the customary oath to the Confederacy he took when he became prosecuting attorney.[4] In short, Baxter was charged with treason. He was soon captured by Confederate General John Marmaduke in southeast Missouri and returned to Little Rock by Colonel R.C. Newton.

Newton and Baxter then became close friends. Newton, whose family had been Whigs, paroled Baxter on his promise to go to Little Rock and report to the Confederate General Theophilus Holmes, who had succeeded Hindman. Newton never expected his friend to fulfill the promise, but Baxter faithfully reported to Little Rock, where his new captors marched him down the streets as a prisoner.[5]

Baxter was imprisoned but never tried. In later years, he said he never felt that the Confederates wanted to bring him to trial. However, Baxter did think he would be shot. After he became governor and the *Arkansas Gazette* became his greatest ally, the paper described his imprisonment and escape:

> He was taken to Little Rock where he remained five months [he was actually in prison from May 1 to August 25], without change of linen and was on the 25th of August to be led out to execution, as he believed, when on the morning of that day, Mrs. Vance, the wife of the heroic Captain Enoch Vance, also in prison for his political views, obtained the keys and turned them [he and Vance] out. He [Baxter] in company with your correspondent, a few days since, in the prison — showed him the cell where he slept the long and gloomy days of his imprisonment, where he kept a chisel and other tools that he vainly thought he could work his way out through a heavy brick wall. On the morning before his liberation by the Christian wife of his friend, in tribulation and sorrow, he received a notification to be ready at 8 o'clock next morning for 'marching orders,' he not knowing whether the march was to be to the scaffold or to the ground where his manner of men were killed by the minnie ball, as he had studied carefully the bill of indictment preferred against him for 'treason to the Confederate States,' which he says, was carefully drawn up. At the time [about 7 o'clock in the morning] Mrs. Vance turned the key to the door of the dungeon that contained her husband and the now governor of Arkansas. He was standing before a bit of broken

glass hung upon the wall, looking upon himself, as he thought for the last time. When the door was thrown open, he and Vance were simply motioned to pass out — not a word was spoken. Deliverance seemed to be at hand. They passed out, walked quietly but, of course, nervously up the public street, separated after going two or three squares [blocks] — Baxter going southwest and Vance going south. Baxter passed through or near a camp of Confederate soldiers, but being dressed so much like them or as a poor, honest countryman, he was not molested, and made for a dense forest, about a half mile distant, where he concealed himself and remained during the day. He says that several times during the day detachments of Confederate cavalry passed near him — within thirty or forty feet — in hot pursuit of the 'traitor.'

He stayed in a cornfield about a mile and a half above town on the bank of the Arkansas River about 16 days, subsisting on green corn without salt — no fires. He then heard guns at Little Rock. A Negro came by and gave him some food and then he saw troops in blue.

The federal troops were across the river. He hollered to them because he thought they were dressed in blue. They explained that Little Rock was in the hands of General Steele. He, in four hours, limped to Markham Street, and fell exhausted. He was taken to General Steele, who placed him in the care of his army hospital and soon in the company of his family.[6]

What strength Baxter must have had to survive eating green corn and drinking muddy river water and swarmed by mosquitoes and other insects. Baxter must have presented a pitiful, unshaven and emaciated sight to this black man, perhaps a slave, for him to share his meager rations. To the Union troops, who later picked him up on Markham Street, he must have appeared as a poor asset to their cause.

After this harrowing experience, Baxter was more willing to fight for the Union, and General Steele authorized him to return to Batesville to recruit and command a regiment of mounted infantry. Baxter complied but his forces were disbanded in the summer of 1864.

Soon Isaac Murphy and other Unionists, including Baxter, formed a loyal government at Little Rock. Baxter became a judge in the Supreme Court of Arkansas and later elected to the U.S. Senate, although the Senate did not recognize his election. After the surrender of the Confederacy, Baxter returned to Batesville and his law practice. That Unionist government was soon superseded by the military directors under the Reconstructin Acts of 1867.

In 1863 Baxter was undoubtedly bitter toward some of the Confederates due to his imprisonment. He filed suit against those who had imprisoned him, but their defense that they were acting on behalf of the Confederate Government was upheld. Baxter expressed in a letter to Governor Isaac Murphy April 12, 1867, his strong views against the rebels and recommended making his fellow prisoner, Vance, governor under the military district bills. [7] Until he became governor, Baxter had been a Powell Clayton Republican but did not behave as a radical.

FOOTNOTES

[1] *Arkansas Gazette*, June 16, 1875.

[2] Clarence Griffin, *History of Old Tryon and Rutherford Counties, North Carolina, 1730-1936* (Asheville, North Carolina, Miller, 1937, pp. 346-347.

[3] Biography by five neighbors at time of his death, now in Arkansas History Commission, Little Rock.

[4] Hindman's friends denied this charge because Judge Ringo signed the warrant for arrest, and Hindman was with General Bragg in Tennessee at that time. Judge Daniel Ringo was the federal judge at Helena before the war and apparently took the same position under the Confederacy. When that section of Arkansas was occupied by the Federals, Lincoln appointed Henry C. Caldwell as Judge, and this proved to be a fine appointment for the Arkansas people.

[5] *Arkansas Gazette*, December 6, 1876, p. 6E.

[6] *Ibid.*, May 17, 1873, 2-2.

[7] Letters in Elisha Baxter file, Arkansas History Commission, Little Rock.

Chapter 10

A Spirit of Fairness and Earnestness

During his inauguration on January 6, 1873, Elisha Baxter delivered a short address, which the *Gazette* stated on January 8, "Breathes a spirit of fairness and earnestness that we have seldom been accustomed to hear from the state executive during the past five years." Over the course of the campaign, the *Gazette* had favored Brooks, supposedly the candidate of the reformers and Democrats. However, at times the paper spoke so kindly of Baxter that many Brooks supporters accused the *Gazette* of being on the other side. Clearly, the *Gazette* would shift support any time it might help get rid of the radicals.

Other conservatives also felt that a new spirit was at hand. The Arkadelphia *Southern Standard* on January 4, 1873, two days before Baxter's inauguration, published a significant statement that the Arkansas people lacked a proper spirit of enterprise, but that the situation was changing.

Baxter encouraged this new enthusiasm by his inaugural words: "I indulge in the hope that the administration to which I am called will mark the commencement of a new era of peace and good feelings in the history of Arkansas."[1]

On December 17, 1872, realizing that Baxter would be inaugurated governor, the *Gazette* said it had never considered Brooks to be a Moses of the conservatives. The paper said Baxter was a "man fully identified with the people of Arkansas; and that if Brooks knew of any fraud, he should bring it to the legislature, not start a fight." With that quotation, the *Gazette* aligned itself with Baxter, at least until he should prove unfaithful to his promise to make a good governor. The paper said it would be free to approve when Baxter made the right move, and free to criticize when he made the wrong one. This paper became influential in many coming struggles.

During the September convention in which Baxter was handed the nomination, he was also given a good platform covering all his promises. Despite leading a corrupt political faction, he at least had the consolation of running on an honest and progressive platform.

Baxter's message to the General Assembly of January 9 sanctioned the end of the rebellion, general good will, equality of all men before the law, early submission of the enfranchisement amendment to vote of the people, better registration, registration books open to the public, the end of circuit superintendents of schools, fewer supreme court judges, lower taxes and more elected officers. Baxter's most significant remark indicated he had undergone some important changes of mind during the campaign:

> . . . banish existing partisan prejudice from our midst, and thereby relieve Arkansas of one of the worst evils with which she has ever been afflicted.

His most promising statement was:

> I shall endeavor to the utmost of my ability to fulfill to the very letter every promise then made [in campaign] . . . in the enactment of all such measures of reform as well curtail our expenditures, and lighten the burden of taxation that is pressing so heavily upon the people.[2]

The people of Arkansas probably would have been happy to have even half of those promises fulfilled. All previous radicals had made similar promises but had been thwarted by violence and corruption. Many Arkansans felt this might be just another such case, but they overlooked the fact that Baxter was an Arkansas Unionist, not a radical.

Charles W. Tankersley was again elected Speaker of the House. He soon announced his committees, composed only of radicals. The election of a U.S. Senator to succeed Senator B.F. Rice was the first job of the General Assembly. The principal candidates were Thomas M. Bowen and Stephen W. Dorsey, both radicals, and Augustus H. Garland, a conservative Democrat. Baxter apparently supported Dorsey,[3] and Clayton apparently supported Bowen, a political ally. Both men kept a low profile during the election. Bowen's strength gradually waned, and Garland's increased, but not enough. With the help of Garland's supporters, Dorsey was elected on January 18. Only 31, he was one of the youngest members of the Senate. The conservative *Gazette* spoke of Dorsey, who had been in Arkansas only a short time:

> While he has been here, however, if he has stolen anything, stuffed any ballot boxes, or been a party to any such conduct, or

in any manner sided or abetted in oppressing the people we have not heard of it.[4]

The buying of Senatorial positions through the General Assemblies of the states was scandalous throughout the nation and many conservatives believed that Dorsey had bought his position.

On January 22, Senator Asa Hodges, a radical from St. Francis County, with the support of John M. Clayton, introduced a bill to punish anyone guilty of usurpation of office.[5] The bill also required that contests begin within 60 days of the election to determine the winners, and the act forbade *quo warranto*, or suit at law compelling an officer to show by what right he held his office. Hodges intended the bill to be a slap at Brooks, who was expected to move against Baxter, and the provision against *quo warranto* was of questionable constitutionality. The bill passed the Senate on a partisan vote. Governor Baxter then signed the bill, perhaps the only radical measure he approved.

Around January 20, the conservatives criticized Baxter for appointing seven untrained blacks as justices of the peace in Ashley County.[6] The *Gazette*, which wanted to pull Baxter away form the radicals, said he could have been misinformed and that it would still give him a chance. Baxter felt kindly toward blacks for the help they gave him when he was in prison. By January 29, Baxter had ordered new registrations in Johnson, Scott, Lawrence, and Greene counties, mostly Brooks's counties. This move pleased most conservatives. The governor indicated he would follow the wishes of the people in his appointments, and many people saw a new light, though still dim, in Arkansas politics.

Perhaps to avoid partisan criticism from the conservative Brooks supporters, the *Gazette* chastised Baxter rather severely for not issuing certificates of election to either the conservative or the radical candidate for Congress in districts one and three. The paper argued that he should have been brave enough to decide one way or the other. Baxter, however, was guided by an earlier case. In 1870, Clayton gave the certificate to John Edwards. Congress promptly overturned that decision and gave the job to Thomas Boles, Edwards's opponent. Baxter therefore wrote out the facts for each side and allowed Congress to decide. In partisan fashion, the House of Representatives seated both radicals.

The previous October, Charles B. Fitzpatrick of Mississippi County had killed J.B. Murray, the county sheriff, and fled across the Mississippi River in a skiff. He refused to return from Tennessee for trial, and the General Assembly passed a bill for the relief of the bondsman and relieving Fitzpatrick from returning for trial.[7]

John M. Clayton, speaking in the Senate for Fitzpatrick,

claimed self defense in the killing. He said Fitzpatrick had made a speech severely criticizing the sheriff. According to Clayton, the sheriff attacked Fitzpatrick with brass knuckles, striking him twice and knocking him to the ground. He was allegedly aiming for the third blow when the prostrate Fitzpatrick drew his gun and killed him.

The governor let the bill become law without his signature primarily because he possibly felt that a mob awaited Fitzpatrick in Mississippi County and that the shooting may have been a legitimate case of self defense.

Fitzpatrick's real character provides an example of the dangerous and irresponsible people who held political offices in this era. As circuit judge, he traveled with a militia corps, and the smaller the county seats where he held court, the more mischievous his behavior became. At Jasper in Newton County, he swaggered about town with his guards and refused to pay either his hotel or his blacksmith bill.[8] Some people accused him of organizing a black society in Mississippi County which intended to kill or run off all the white citizens in the community and charging big fees for his leadership. When Fitzpatrick killed Murray, his army of blacks fought with the whites and lost three men.[9]

After becoming governor, Baxter resigned as judge of the third circuit. Unannounced, the radicals under Justice McClure's control sent him a successor, a Mr. McCulloch.[10] The governor decided that McCulloch did not qualify and appointed James W. Butler on March 10.

Even though McClure testified that he never approved of the nomination of Baxter in the previous year, this marked the beginning of an open war between the two — a conflict enhanced by McClure's editorials in the *Republican*.

This refusal of Baxter to allow the radicals to send him men to be appointed to leading positions was his first conflict with them, and he handled it in a statesman-like manner. As Clayton's hatchet man, McClure was through.

Up to that point, few serious matters had come before the General Assembly, and Baxter had proposed no innovative programs. Many days the Assembly tried to adjust county lines or find excess territory in several adjoining counties from which the members could carve a county to be named Sherman. Lincoln, Grant, and Clayton Counties had been created by the two previous General Assemblies.

On March 26 George Latta, a conservative from the 13th District, finally asked, "How many times are Republicans allowed to vote on this floor?"

A voice answered, "As many times as they desire; it is perfectly natural."

W.H. Furbush, a black from Phillips County who had the support of many whites, moved that "this mob adjourn." Furbush had been trying for weeks to pass a bill creating Coolidge County, named for a prominent philanthropist from Phillips County. He had encountered a series of parliamentary entanglements, his bill had been stolen or locked up, and he was tired of this shabby treatment.

The chair ruled that the bill needed engrossment. Angered by the ruling, Furbush replied, "Then with the consent of the House, I withdraw this G-d d-d bill."

Representative Millen moved that Furbush be expelled. "I wish you would expel me," Furbush responded. "I am tired of the whole G-d d-d legislature."[11] At that point, Furbush said, "I will be glad to be expelled, and I never want my name used in connection with this G-d d-d legislature again." He came to the bar with his coat on his arm and his hat in his hand. Mr. Beasley, who was rapidly becoming a conservative leader, wanted Furbush to remain and moved that the House adjourn. His motion carried ending the matter.

On the same day, the Senate discussed a bill not to require one-legged men to work on the roads. In short, this General Assembly, brought to the office by the same political machine that elected Baxter, became the most disgraceful in Arkansas history. Baxter explained to the Poland Committee of Congress which investigated Arkansas in 1874 that he had to watch this irresponsible legislature closely.[12]

A civil rights bill for blacks passed February 21 and Baxter signed it, but unfortunately few people paid any attention to the act because they correctly thought the law would not be enforced. The February 28 *Gazette* commented:

> We cannot but hide our heads in shame when we think that our state has sunk so low as to have a mob like this to legislate for us.

Up to this time, Baxter had been a different governor than either Clayton or Hadley. He had been a middle-of-the-road governor who favored neither side. The General Assembly had not hurried in its work, and Baxter had not tried to hurry the legislative body. Clayton still felt that on important issues he would control Baxter.

Perhaps the most significant bill passed by the General Assembly under Baxter was one approving an amendment to the 1868 Constitution that enfranchised all those participating in the war and providing for an election March 3 to vote on the amendment. The measure had been approved by the previous General Assembly, but amendments required the approval of two consecutive sessions. At that time, about 500 Arkansans were disfranchised under the federal acts, but about a third of the whites, or roughly 20,000, were disfranchised under the state acts. No one of importance on either side opposed the measure, and the vote, which was light, carried 25,199 for to 3,695 against.[13] However, the amendment lost in the predominantly black county of Chicot 51 to 363, and several other heavily black counties voted against it.[14] This Arkansas amendment, however, had two words that could be dangerous — "if registered." The registration system allowed the governor to appoint and dismiss all registrars, who were empowered to refuse to register anyone they deemed disloyal and to report the results as they pleased. Everything then depended on the governor, and Baxter's remarks about honest elections would have alarmed the radicals had they not felt that they could control him. To the consternation of the radicals, Elisha Baxter gave every indication that he intended to conduct fair elections.

A strange silence and inactivity settled over the General Assembly by early March, and some people began to criticize the legislature for doing nothing and wasting taxpayers' money. The legislators, however, began discussing the railroad bond situation, which indicated that something might be brewing behind the scenes. Charles Brown, representative from the Ninth District (Crittenden, St. Francis, and Woodruff counties), introduced a bill to stop issuing any more railroad bonds. This measure brought the railroad situation to the forefront even though the radicals defeated the bill.

On March 30, Benton Turner of Conway County introduced another major railroad bill. The measure amended the railroad act of July 21, 1868, which authorized the state to aid the railroads with construction bonds in the amount of $10,000 per mile for those roads given government land grants and $15,000 per mile for those not receiving land grants or a total of $11,400,000. The state issued the bonds and delivered them to the railroads as the tracks were constructed, and $5,200,000 had been issued up to this time. The railroads were supposed to pay the bonds, but if they did not, they became the obligation of the state, and the state was authorized to take over any railroad whenever it got behind on its bonds.[15]

The proposed bill contained a clause providing that the state relieve the railroads of payment because they were poor security for the bonds, and the state would take that much stock in each railroad in lieu of those bond payments. The issuance of additional stock would have watered the stock, and the state would have been swapping mortgages for nearly worthless stock further watered down.

In addition, a three-mill state-wide property tax was to be levied to pay the interest and principal on the bonds. Since the property assessment exceeded $100 million, this would bring $300,000 per year restoring the bonds to par. The radicals called for immediate passage of the bill before news of its contents could reach over the state.

Immediately, X.J. Pindall, a conservative from Desha County, "to test the sense of the House on this gigantic steal," moved that the bill be rejected, but the motion failed 28 to 41. Pindall's remark, however, named the bill — thereafter it was known to both supporters and opponents as "the railroad steal bill." The radicals had the votes to pass the bill, and they also owned a lot of the railroad stock and many of the bonds and held many high positions in the companies.

Mr. Sarber, a leading radical from Johnson County, moved to suspend the rules to eliminate the second reading, but his motion lost, indicating that some radicals feared pushing the bill through too fast. Opposition to the bill developed over-night, led by the *Gazette* and including a majority of the non-radical papers over the state. However, eventually even some of the staunchest Republican papers, including the Helena *World*, opposed it. [16] The *Republican* took an expected radical view in criticizing Baxter: "We are getting sick of this one-man [Baxter] power. It [the power] was given to the executive to hold the Republican Party in power."

The opposition in the General Assembly seemed too weak to defeat the bill, and consequently much depended upon Baxter. Prior decisions of his were child's play, but this was one which would stamp him forever as a partner of the thieves, or a champion of the debt-ridden people of Arkansas. Only the governor could save the situation. Just as the Kansas-Nebraska Bill had divided the nation into two irreconcilable camps in 1854, this bill did the same to Arkansas. The immediate associations of Governor Baxter with those who opposed the bill let the conservatives know that they had a champion. He did not announce through the press that he would veto the bill, but the legislators knew that he would.

This was a watershed decision for Baxter. He opposed the bill and thereafter became an enemy of the radicals. Overnight the politics of Arkansas took a 180-degree turn. Conservatives became pro-Baxter, and radicals anti-Baxter.

On April 3 the bill passed the House 36 to 26, and then went to the Senate. McClure announced that four Republicans, including two blacks, J.T. White and G.H. Stewart from the Eleventh District of Phillips and Monroe counties, had abandoned the cause. White, a preacher, answered that if he ever went to hell, he would be doubly disgraced if he found that he was under John McClure instead of the devil.[17]

About this bill, the conservative Helena *World* stated:
... Now we glance at the murderous movement, which seems almost on the verge of triumph. We are well nigh led to say, all is ended, swayed, sunk, lost, forever cursed.

From all over the nation came comments concerning the bill, and the Senate tried to amend it to meet some of the objections. It changed the word "stock" to "preferred stock." The Senate eliminated the three-mill tax for the payment of the bonds, although the bonds would still remain the state's obligations.[18] The opposition pointed out that the three-mill tax could be passed again later, for a state debt would have to be funded.

This weakened bill then passed the Senate April 9 by a vote of 14 to 12. The measure went back to the House for acceptance of the amendments and there rested while the opposition grew and the hour for adjournment drew closer. If the House should accept the Senate changes and then adjourn, the governor would have a great advantage of a pocket veto that could not be overridden. The House did not accept this amended version, but sent it back to the Senate where it was passed again on April 24 by a vote of 15 to 7. On the morning of adjournment, April 25, the House refused to consider the amended bill by a vote of 26 to 51, which showed the rapidly growing power of public opinion. The governor therefore did not have to veto a bill which everyone by then knew that he would. Thus Governor Baxter stood in a dangerous position squarely with the people and against the powerful ring which elected him. Baxter's second crisis stamped him well.

W.W. Wilshire, a carpetbagger in Congress being challenged by Thomas Gunter, a Fayetteville Democrat, wrote to the Arkansas press that he wrote the original railroad bill of 1868, but that the money had not been used to build railroads as intended but to buy favors from politicians and send men to places of summer amusement. He said he had supported Baxter in the 1872 campaign, and, after Baxter's stand against the steal bill, he was a more enthusiastic supporter than ever.[19] This stand by Wilshire switched him permanently into the conservative ranks.

Baxter's stand on the steal bill won the governor an enthusiastic response throughout the state. A prominent journalist who signed "Au Revoir" wrote in the Fort Smith *Tri-Weekly Herald* April 26 that "Baxter, through it all, has conducted himself with a manly firmness that I did not think was in him." The *Herald* then became a supporter of Baxter.

"Au Revoir" also outlined the three major plans of the radicals.[20] First, the writer indicated the radicals wanted the railroad steal bill, which lay dead in the House. Secondly, they wanted an election bill which would have placed election control in the hands of the lieutenant governor (Volney V. Smith), the auditor (Stephen Wheeler), and the treasurer (Henry Page), all Clayton-McClure supporters. Baxter helped defeat the bill, which became known as the V.V. Smith bill.[21] The third measure in the radical plan was the metropolitan police bill, which would have placed all law enforcement power in the hands of the radicals, creating a commission of the lieutenant governor, auditor and treasurer. The radicals never pushed these last two bills because the governor said he would veto them.

In the furor over the railroad steal bill, these other two were overlooked, and when the metropolitan police bill was taken up in the House on April 4, opponents condemned the act as dictatorial and let it die.

Two rumors surfaced during the career of these three bills — that the railroads offered the radicals $500,000 to pass the steal bill, cancelling a debt of $5,200,000 and an additional $6,200,000 eligible for issue, and that the ring also planned another $400,000 appropriation for further payment for theft and destruction of property by the militia. Since nearly all of the first $125,000 for militia damages was stolen, this looked like more easy money. When they couldn't pass the first three bills, they abandoned this one. Most of the $500,000 would have been paid to themselves since they were big stockholders in the railroads.

Ex-governor Clayton became unhappy over the failure of these bills and a rift between Clayton and Baxter appeared inevitable. Clayton gave an indication of his relationship with Baxter in an interview with the New York *Times* on May 22, 1873. He had returned to his hotel in Washington, D.C., and Hadley was with him:

Clayton denied that he would try to replace Baxter with force; that Baxter was well regarded in Arkansas; that he knew that Baxter was properly elected governor, even though the Democrats claimed that Brooks was elected; that Brooks' right to contest the election had to be approved by both houses of the General Assembly, but he got only nine votes in the House on a motion to that effect, even though they had elected 34 members, that Democrats were rapidly deserting Brooks; that Baxter's gains with the Democrats was due to his appointment of members of that party to offices, and that Baxter feared that Brooks or his friends would start a *quo warranto* suit against him, and that he and Baxter remained friends, but that the Democrats were trying to win him over to their party as their leader instead of Brooks.

Clayton admitted that Baxter was losing out with the Republicans, and against his [Clayton's] advice wanted to replace D.P. Upham from head of the militia with these new Democratic friends. He told how he [Clayton] went to the capitol, and guards hollered, 'Who goes there?' and that he found the governor surrounded by ex-Confederate soldiers. He regretted that he had selected Baxter as their candidate, but he had to do so as no carpetbagger could have been elected.

In reality, ex-Confederates and conservatives (Democrats or Republicans) had flocked to Baxter and the radicals had shifted to Brooks. Even northwest Arkansas, a Unionist strong-hold which had supported Brooks, began to swing to Baxter by the summer. In June, the Harrison newspaper declared, "Baxter now man of the people."[22] Chief Justice John McClure understood the situation better than Clayton, and began working with other radicals to remove Baxter by quasi-legal methods. The Daily *Republican*, then under McClure's control, wrote:

> Down with one-man power. It is time a lesson was taught the man who would thwart the will of the party. We say, strike at the root, and never cease striking until this contumacy and this pigheadishness has been taught its first lesson.[23]

The *Gazette* had previously liked Baxter and gradually became his standard bearer, leading the Democratic press in his favor. Only the Fayetteville *Democrat* and the Fort Smith *Tri-Weekly Herald*, among leading conservative papers, did not accept Baxter's leadership. However, even these two papers fought the steal bill.

On March 7, the *Gazette* summarized the state's financial condition and revealed that the total bonded debt had touched twenty million dollars including bonds appropriated but not sold. An additional half million of auditor's warrants (scrip) was outstanding[24] as was a half million dollars in delinquent interest on the bonds as of January 1, 1873. This debt equaled a fifth of the total assessed valuation of the taxable property in Arkansas.[25]

The total tax rate on property by all governments was 5 per cent or 50 mills, but the current expenses of the state exceeded the tax income. A legislator sought to relieve the situation by introducing a bill for the governor to issue two million dollars in 7 per cent bonds of $1,000 each, payable in New York in gold coins of the U.S. government. The governor, lieutenant governor, and auditor were to serve as committee to decide each year how many such bonds to issue, and when to issue them, and to decide their market value. The expenses of the General Assembly were to be covered by the first issue, and holders of scrip could trade for bonds. An additional tax of 1½ mills was to be levied to fund the bonds. The *Gazette* pointed out that after two years, a supplemental bond issue would be necessary, and that the state debt would grow by refunding alone and by selling bonds under par.

This session of the General Assembly had continued for four months and cost $270,000. Along with financial problems, the legislature created an unprecedented nine new counties including one named in Governor Baxter's honor.

The creation of these new counties brought new circuit court judgeships and minor positions, giving the governor about 300 new appointments. Elisha Baxter did exactly what the previous two governors had done — strengthen himself with appointments, but he appointed people who he thought would serve honorably whether they were Republicans, Democrats, old-line Southerners, or Unionists.

The General Assembly did pass several pieces of constructive legislation: the appropriation of $1,000 to restore a Catholic church in southwest Arkansas destroyed by the Catterson militia in 1868, the establishment of a state college for blacks at Pine Bluff, and the election of sheriffs instead of appointment by the governor.

Despite the passage of these positive measures, the House became unruly on the last day. As someone shouted, "Order, order," he crashed through a window on the east end of the hall. When one member introduced a bill to punish drunkards, another bellowed, "Don't be so hard on us." The chair asked for quiet but was greeted by shouts of "Go to hell," "Quit eating peanuts," "It's my right," and "Shut up." By accident, the speaker made a prophetic remark. When someone asked him to prevent the members from leaving, he remarked, "We will all soon go out, never to return." Someone moved "that the mob adjourn," and they walked out without ceremony.

The behavior of this General Assembly and Baxter's aloofness to it are explained by his testimony to the Poland Committee (later explained) as appears on page 414 of *Affairs in Arkansas*, the Congressional Report of that committee: Baxter: "In fact, I am not very social in my habits, anyhow. But I confess to you that I became completely and utterly disgusted at a large proportion of the Republican members of the Legislature; so much so that, so far as I now remember, I was but once during the whole sitting of the Legislature in the Hall of Representatives and but once in the Senate Chamber ... It was because of my utter disgust at their manner and course of proceedings."

FOOTNOTES

[1] Arkadelphia *Southern Standard*, January 11, 1873, 1-6.
[2] *Arkansas Gazette*, January 10, 1873, 1-1.
[3] Poland Report, p. 515.
[4] *Arkansas Gazette*, January 19, 1873, 2-2.
[5] *Ibid.*, January 23, 1873, 1-1.
[6] *Ibid.*, January 24, 1873, 2-2.
[7] *Ibid.*, March 1, 1873, 1-1.
[8] *Arkansas Gazette*, August 11, 1871, August 30, 1871, 2-2, and September 6, 1871, 1-1.
[9] *Ibid.*, October 23, 1872, and Arkadelphia *Southern Standard*, October 26, 1872, 1-6.
[10] Poland Report, p. 410.
[11] *Journal of the Arkansas House of Representatives*, March 26, 1873.
[12] Poland Report, p. 413.
[13] *Arkansas Gazette*, September 20, 1873, New York *Times*, October 30, 1873, 1-1.
[14] *Ibid.*, September 22, 1873, 2-2.
[15] Fayetteville *Democrat*, March 28, 1873, 1-3. *Arkansas Gazette*, April 1, 1873, 2-1.
[16] *Arkansas Gazette*, April 12, 1873, 1-2.
[17] *Ibid.*, April 10, 1873, 1-1.
[18] *Ibid.*, April 10, 1873, 1-1.
[19] *Ibid.*, June 17, 1873, 2-3.
[20] *Ibid.*, June 17, 1873, 2-3.
[21] *Journal of the Senate of Arkansas*, March 13, 1873.
[22] Boone County *Highlander*, June 14, 1873, 2-2.
[23] New York *Times*, May 22, 1873, 5-1.
[24] Letter from Arkansas History Commission to author October 14, 1981, indicates much more than this amount of scrip was issued.
[25] *Arkansas Gazette*, March 7, 1873, 2-1.

Chapter 11

The Two-Edged Sword of Elisha Baxter

Joseph Brooks received no help from Clayton in his first efforts to take the governor's office from Baxter. Clayton wanted no rival and hoped to get rid of Baxter and replace him with the compliant lieutenant governor, Volney Voltaire Smith.

When Baxter was sworn in as governor January 6, 1873, Brooks applied to the Federal District Court at Helena for an order declaring himself the properly elected governor. Judge Henry C. Caldwell ruled on January 11 that since the question did not involve a federal question under the Fifteenth Amendment to the U.S. Constitution or in the Federal Enforcement Act, the whole thing was a matter for the state to decide. Judge Caldwell had previously made a similar decision in a contest of an election to the Arkansas Supreme Court.[1] Caldwell, appointed by Lincoln, had been a federal army officer serving in Arkansas but was not a radical and was well liked by the Southern people.

On April 18, 1873, Mr. C. Thrower, the representative from the 19th District (Ouachita and Nevada Counties), introduced a measure in the House authorizing Brooks to contest Baxter's election. By this time, the railroad bond steal bill had died, and Brooks hoped to get the support of those radicals who had turned against Baxter for his prominent part in defeating the bill. Harrell (p. 196) stated that the radicals fell from Baxter like leaves from a tree in autumn. The *Gazette* counted 22 radicals who had shifted to Brooks, but the Thrower bill met defeat by a count of 29 to 36. The vote should have told Brooks that he was losing strength from the conservatives faster than he was gaining from the radicals and that a shift in allegiance was occurring on both sides.

Brooks, however, asked again in a long, eloquent speech to be heard. The petition for a contest including testimony was denied April 18, 63 to 9.

It was rumored that if the General Assembly allowed Brooks to contest Baxter's election, the state Supreme Court, which was composed of Clayton supporters, would declare the office of governor vacant until the case ended. They would then adjourn the General Assembly so the case would not be decided until the next elected General Assembly met as provided by the Constitution, and Lieutenant Governor Smith would serve until a new General Assembly took over. Under that arrangement the next election would be controlled by Clayton, but the ex-governor's supporters realized late in the session that Baxter was strengthening himself with his appointments. The *Gazette* chided Brooks, as well as Bowen, who lost their senatorial races, that they created in the Constitutional Convention of 1868 this executive power which then had turned against both of them.[2]

The Senate, which had confirmation power over many appointments, then began rejecting Baxter's selections. The move was too late, however, for Baxter had already appointed many people without objection. The General Assembly then adjourned, leaving Baxter free to appoint whomever he pleased until the next session. He made a total of 331 appointments.[3] Baxter was also quietly requiring many undated letters of resignation from his appointees to use if necessary. However, he never accepted or used one.[4] Many appointments needed no Senate confirmation under the sweeping powers of the governor's office, and consequently, the sword of battle which the radicals had forged was double edged, and Baxter began swinging it effectively against his opponents.

The legislature adjourned April 25, and the *Gazette* noted that "Baxter could now operate without the legislature around his neck; that he had but two courses to pursue: to decide with the people and destroy the ring or desert the people and side with the ring."[5]

Governor Baxter felt the pressure from the radicals who had elected him, and he prepared for the worst. Not only did Brooks want the courts to declare Baxter's election invalid, but rumors circulated over the state that McClure wanted to remove Baxter by legal legerdemain or by a coup and place Lieutenant Governor V.V. Smith in the governorship.

Baxter removed all his enemies from the militia and appointed his friends. On May 15, 1873, he removed General Upham and appointed ex-Confederate General T.J. Churchill head of the Eastern Department. He appointed General Thomas P. Dockery commander of the Western Department, and placed R.C. Newton under him. Both men were former Confederate generals. He also placed some cadets of St. John's Military College and some citizens as guards of the State House, showing how seriously he considered the possibility of an armed rebellion or an assassination attempt.[6]

A writer who signed "Judex" reported in the Fort Smith *Herald* May 24 that "McClure had had plans of a coup by an armed force, but Governor Baxter formed an armed guard of 100 men under John C. Peay and was able to hold the capitol."[7] In testimony in Poland's investigations, John Peay affirmed that guns had been stolen from the armory, and that Governor Baxter asked him to form a guard to protect the Capitol where the guns were stored. He and about 40 or 50 guards stayed there around six nights to guard the guns. Peay was head of the cadets of St. John and a prominent Democrat and supporter of Baxter, and the armed guard was the above-mentioned cadets reinforced by a few volunteers from Little Rock. But no evidence has been found that McClure had a strong force or that Clayton then approved of a coup which, it was rumored, McClure planned.

The *Gazette* on May 16, 17, 21, and 22, page 1 and column 1 of every issue gave this story in more detail and later stated that Baxter ate and slept in his Capitol room, and rarely went out unguarded.[8]

The same paper stated on May 24:
If Governor Baxter can expel this den of vipers from political position, he will receive the everlasting gratitude of the honest people of all parties.[9]

Brooks, after his defeat in the General Assembly, returned to the courts. On June 2, T.W.D. Yonley, aided by Attorney General John R. Montgomery, filed with the Supreme Court on behalf of Brooks a suit against Baxter, the complaint stating: "who for over three months [the papers had been drawn up in April] has held, used, and executed the said office of governor without any legal warrant, grant, or right whatsoever."[10] Baxter was defended by Judge Elbert H. English. The New York *Times* stated:
Although positive statements were made not long since by prominent Republicans of Arkansas [Clayton among them] that no purpose was entertained to disturb Governor Baxter in his position, the Attorney General has applied for a writ of *quo warranto* for his ejectment, on the grounds that he has usurped the office. This proceeding seems to us not only an act of bad faith but revolutionary. Governor Baxter gives notice, in advance, that he denies the jurisdiction of the court, and will pay no attention to its decree, in all of which he is justified by the late assertions of his present opponents. In any well-regulated community it would be safe to assume that such an

application, under the circumstances which surround the case of Governor Baxter, would be denied, but it is not safe to assume anything in Arkansas. Governor Baxter has doubtless done much to forfeit the confidence of his former supporters, but there has been nothing in his conduct to justify the course which seems to have been determined upon to get rid of him. The Republicans of the state cannot expect the public to have any sympathy with a movement which many of themselves have declared to be illegal, unnecessary, and disastrous to the peace and prosperity of the state.[11]

On June 3 Clayton wired Baxter that the suit had been filed without his concent and that he believed Baxter to be the rightful governor of Arkansas. "I hope you will stand firm regardless of the results." On June 4 the Court ruled against Brooks 3 to 1, with only McClure dissenting and one justice not voting. Clayton apparently still hoped to pull Baxter under his influence and was willing to let the radical-dominated Court leave him in office.[12]

To ask Baxter to not organize or use the militia until after trouble had begun was particularly hypocritical. Baxter, in taking the position he did, had clearly stymied the radicals in their endeavors to control Arkansas.

In general, many people continued to approve of Baxter's appointments and decisions, and Baxter made large gains among the conservative whites, especially ex-Confederates.[13]

Baxter appointed the brother-in-law of Augustus H. Garland, Confederate Captain John Bull, as sheriff of Hempstead County. Bull succeeded James Vance, who had resigned after making exaggerated reports of black mob rule.[14]

On the night of June 9, 1873, the guards around the Capitol, followed by a crowd of citizens, serenaded Baxter, who spoke to them:

> Fellow citizens, when, a few months ago, I swore upon the Holy Evangelist to execute faithfully and impartially the duties of the high office with which I was invested and entrusted, I made no idle or unmeaning vow which I might discard as interest and convenience might suggest . . . I could not have acted otherwise without compromising my selfrespect, and making me an object of contempt to my own better feelings and interests . . . I intend never to deviate in any important particular from the strict line of policy marked out by the tenets and doctrines of my party. I am a republican, not only in name but in principle, and would like to hold fellowship with all who practice as well as profess the principles of that party.[15]

Brooks had not finished fighting. Eleven days after the Supreme Court decision, he applied in Pulaski County Circuit Court for a writ of possession for the office of governor and the salary paid to Baxter.[16] Due to the Supreme Court decision, Judge John Whytock deferred action to the next term of court. This decision to defer rather than throw out the case may have been dictated by Clayton in order to hold it over Baxter's head since he preferred Baxter over Brooks.

Brooks passed out handbills announcing he would speak at the Grand Opera House in Little Rock on the evening of June 27. He had a large crowd of Brindles (Brooks Republicans), minstrels,[17] and blacks, but few conservatives. He spoke for three hours. He reviewed the fight for liberty in the past centuries in Europe and scorned the *Gazette* and Elisha Baxter. He compared Powell Clayton favorably to Baxter. If he got a judgment in Whytock's court, he said, he would qualify and take the office. "Give me liberty or give me death," he exclaimed as he closed. It was his greatest oratorical effort,[18] and the ladies in the audience threw him bouquets. He left a clear impression that he might try to take the office by force if and when Whytock ruled in his favor.

Baxter never attempted to answer such oratorical demonstrations, but the *Gazette* said:

> Brooks is the chronic agitator of the age. To be compelled to keep silent would be death to him. We propose to give him enough rope and let him hang himself, as he will be sure to do in the end.[19]

Baxter later admitted to the Poland committee[20] that he never intended to obey any decision of the Supreme Court regarding his tenure of office since the constitution of 1868 gave that authority entirely to the legislature.

It was also clear from his many remarks that Brooks might welcome a combination with Clayton to displace Baxter.

FOOTNOTES

[1] New York *Times*, January 14, 1873, 1-6.
[2] *Arkansas Gazette*, January 26, 1873, 2-2.
[3] Little Rock *Republican*, August 12, 1873.
[4] *Affairs in Arkansas*, (Poland Report) p. 415.
[5] *Arkansas Gazette*, April 29, 1873, 2-2.
[6] *Ibid.*, May 16, 1873, 1-1.
[7] New York *Times*, May 18, 1873, 2-2, and Poland Report, pp. 408-9.
[8] *Arkansas Gazette*, May 24, 1873, 2-2, and New York *Times*, May 18, 1873, 2-2.
[9] *Arkansas Gazette*, May 27, 1873, 1-1.
[10] *Ibid.*, May 5, 1873, 4-4.
[11] New York *Times*, April 16, 1874, 5-5, 17th, 5-1, 18th, 7-1, and 19th, 1-5.
[12] Fayetteville *Democrat*, June 14, 1873. *Arkansas Gazette*, June 4, 1873, 1-1, and June 5, 1873, 4-4.

[13] *Arkansas Gazette*, June 10, 1873, 1-2.
[14] Arkadelphia *Southern Standard*, June 4, 1873, 1-6.
[15] *Arkansas Gazette*, June 10, 1873, 4-4.
[16] New York *Times*, June 29, 1873, 4-2, *Arkansas Gazette*, June 18, 1873, 1-1.
[17] The term "minstrel" has seldom been used in this study. It refers to the Clayton radicals, because John R. Price, one of the first of Clayton supporters, had a minstrel troup before he came to Arkansas. Both terms came from street gossip.
[18] *Arkansas Gazette*, June 28, 1873, 1-1.
[19] *Ibid.*, June 29, 1873, 2-2 & 3.
[20] Poland Report, p. 421.

Chapter 12

Brooks's Line of March

The leading Southerners fell out with Brooks rapidly, and U.M. Rose, the noted Arkansas attorney, wrote Harris Flanigan on September 3, 1873: "But Mr. Brooks and his body guards have so treated me that I hope that they will soon take up their line of march, and it is generally believed they will . . ." "Line of march" meant a shooting line of march — in short, an armed revolution against the Baxter government of Arkansas. Before that date, Rose had been close to neutral, but he was leaning toward Baxter.

A multitude of suggestions had been made by various people to resolve Arkansas's troubles. First, a new constitution should be written; second, a new election for governor should be held if it could be done constitutionally. And finally, that all members of the General Assembly should resign and a new group elected following a new registration that would include those recently granted amnesty by the constitutional amendment.[1] The new legislature could decide matters, and Baxter had every reason to believe that the people would elect those favorable to him.

In July, August, and September, a few legislators resigned, and Baxter gave them better jobs. By October, members, primarily Republicans, resigned almost daily, and Baxter appointed nearly all of them to state and county positions. During the last session nine new counties were formed. This development provided a multitude of new officers for Baxter to appoint — a great political advantage for him.

The Fayetteville *Democrat* thought better of Baxter than did the leading politicians of Northwest Arkansas. However, the paper contended that Brooks had actually won the election. An editorial on July 5, 1873 said:

It matters not that Mr. Baxter has done some praiseworthy

deeds — it matters not that he had made some good appointments — it matters not that with pious cant he tells of his reverence for the interests of the people — all this will avail nothing when we are confronted with the great stubborn fact which looms up above all facts, that he was not elected, and holds office by a monstrous fraud upon the people.

The *Gazette* addressed this nagging question August 21:
Did Baxter receive a majority of the votes? That's the question we do not propose to attempt to decide... It is not our function to determine it. He was declared elected by the proper tribunal by a majority of 3,111 over Brooks...
Certain it is, however, that in several counties very grave frauds were committed by the friends of Mr. Brooks, by which Mr. Baxter was defrauded of numerous votes...
Mr. Baxter holds the office of governor through the only means known to the law for inducting an official of that character into the position. He did not appoint the registrars. He did not make the returns. He did not publish the results, nor did he have any agency in all this. He took upon himself the duties of governor after being duly declared elected, just as any other citizen of the state would have done.

Robert Johnson, former U.S. Senator who had led Arkansas into secession, initially supported Brooks in the election. However, he soon became a Baxter convert. "I care not how Baxter was elected; he is our savior now," he wrote in a letter to the *Gazette*. Many voters shared this position.[2]

It became apparent to numerous Arkansas people by the middle of 1873 that both the McClure radicals and Brooks's forces were attacking Baxter, not each other. Baxter was gaining strength daily among conservatives of both parties. Former Republican Circuit Judge Liberty Bartlett of Little Rock later explained to the Poland Committee that "The Democrats flocked to Baxter because (1) Baxter held the office of Governor, and (2) he did everything both he and Brooks had promised to do."

To achieve any future union, the opponents of Baxter had to refute Brooks's accusation that the radical Republicans had stolen the election. Therefore, the radical press began claiming that if the election was stolen (and possibly it was) Baxter did the stealing.

The Clayton-McClure-Hadley machine controlled most of the Arkansas government in 1872, including the registrars and election commissioners. They mailed election results from the counties to the secretary of state, who turned them over to the President of the Senate, as required by law. The President of the Senate, Volney Voltaire Smith, and his associates then handled the matter.

In the late summer of 1873, the rumors of a shooting conflict between the McClure radicals and the Baxter forces became so pronounced that U.S. Attorney General Williams recommended that Governor Baxter call for federal troops to maintain order. Baxter made the request, and President Grant offered protection in a letter of September 25. W.W. Wilshire and R.C. Newton, both major generals in the Arkansas Militia, offered their resignations on the 29th to clear the way for the federals.[3]

In conferring with Governor Baxter, Wilshire and Newton suggested that fighting the rebellion with militia would bring on civil strife and that perhaps federal troops could do a better job. The governor accepted the resignations on the following day and then disbanded the entire militia except for the adjutant general and the personal staff of the commander-in-chief. This complete disbanding of the militia was a mistake, for Baxter needed some close guards under his personal direction.

In late September, influential Clayton radicals, in order to make peace with Baxter, purchased McClure's interest in the Little Rock *Republican*.[4] McClure, as chief editorial writer, had been most abusive of the governor. The paper's new policy took effect about October 1 and other radical papers followed the *Republican's* lead. On October 6, the *Republican* reprinted an article from the radical *White River Journal*:

> Both political parties have committed great and unpardonable errors ... At last we behold the gleamings of the morn which ushers in the new era of peace and prosperity ... Governor Baxter has disbanded his militia.

As further proof that Clayton's followers wanted peace with Baxter, the Republican Central Committee on October 8 publicly stated that "Governor Baxter's tenure of the office he holds is fixed and irrevocable." This 500-word document was signed by Clayton, chairman; U.S. Senator Dorsey; O.A. Hadley, and other leading radicals. W.W. Wilshire, a Republican supporter of Baxter, wrote the *Republican* a similar letter.[5] Because of this support, the rumors of rebellion beginning in May died down as rapidly as they had arisen.

Another rumor spread over the state in early fall that Baxter had sold out to Clayton, and many people became alarmed that the radicals would return to power. To combat the allegations, on October 7 the *Gazette* published a letter from R.C. Newton to the conservative Senator B.B. Beavers of Benton affirming that Governor Baxter had told him he would not resign to take a lucrative federal job, thus leaving Lieutenant Governor Volney V. Smith as governor.

Baxter, however, demonstrated that he could play another

game that Clayton and Hadley had played. On June 12 the *Gazette* announced that Baxter had given the paper the state printing for Pulaski County. This announcement was a major blow to the radicals, because the radical papers had previously received all the legal advertising. Since they had little paid circulation, the state advertising had been their major source of income. An investigation in 1874 revealed that the *Republican* received $157,000 from the state during the four-month session of the 1873 General Assembly.[6] Later in the year other friendly and conservative papers over the state began to share in this political plum, and one by one the radical papers ceased publication.

On September 18, 1873 Baxter called for an election to be held on November 4 to determine successors to the 47 members of the General Assembly who had resigned.[7] After that election, the conservatives had 54 representatives to the radicals' 28, and eleven senators to the radicals' fifteen, a huge increase in conservative representation. The election showed Baxter's growing popularity with the Arkansas people. The radicals were alarmed by the gains of the pro-Baxter forces because they had enough support in the House to defeat any bill and prevent impeachment.

Businesswise, Arkansas advanced rapidly, despite the political unrest and the great national financial panic of late 1873. The Cairo and Fulton Railroad, which declined to accept the state bond assistance of $3,000,000, crossed the Arkansas River at Little Rock on December 22, 1873[8] and completed a bridge across the Red River at Fulton the following March. The railroad crossed the state diagonally from the northeast to the southwest and connected with railroads that went both east and west. It became the greatest railroad of the state and soon was incorporated into the larger Missouri Pacific system.

Partly due to this prosperity, beginning in October, 1873, the animosity between Baxter and his enemies lessened. The Little Rock *Republican* for several years had been controlled by Justice John McClure, even though John Price was the titular editor.[9] It did not take long for McClure to understand that Governor Baxter was independent of the Clayton machine. The *Republican*, under McClure, attacked Baxter viciously throughout the summer of 1873, calling him a liar, a spineless eunuch, a prisoner of the Ku Klux Klan, and a usurper, among other things.

The Supreme Court decided in Baxter's favor on June 4, 1873.[10] It was noted later that the decision had not been entered on the court records, and pro-Baxter people became worried. Justice Stephenson kept the decision in his pocket, and at one time it was intimated to Baxter that the decision might not be filed unless he held to the radical program. When McClure left the Little Rock *Republican*, the decision was filed and peace overtures were extended to Baxter in the form of favorable press coverage beginning October 1. The *Republican* accepted the court decision and on October 6 wrote: "Both political parties have committed great and unpardonable errors... McClure and his Republican party wing have closed their war upon the executive. Baxter is and will remain the governor of Arkansas." The paper then praised Baxter for his adherence to the Republican platform and sympathized with him for being slandered by his enemies.

The *Gazette* observed this turnabout and said on February 12, 1874: "The Arkansas war is closed. We trust our readers will sleep more quietly after this announcement." This had become a typical pattern during Reconstruction: a crisis, followed by a quiet spell, only to be broken again by a new outburst. By this time the four radicals who ran for U.S. Representative were all declared elected by the radically controlled House on a partisan vote. However, W.W. Wilshire was not radical enough and was seated only temporarily by a vote of 135 to 129.

Another incident which pointed toward political peace was the death of Charles Sumner on March 11, 1874.[11] He had succeeded Daniel Webster in the U.S. Senate upon his appointment as Secretary of State in 1851, and for over 20 years his career was distinguished by passionate speeches against slavery. He was a friend of the freedman, but his elements of greatness were often smothered by his passions, and his death signaled a possible end of vigorous anti-Southern Congressional pressure.

In state circles, the victory of the conservatives under Elisha Baxter was complete. From the *Monticellonian* in southeast Arkansas, formerly a radical publication, came the glad message:

> Our experience with radicalism is too great... The manly strokes of Governor Baxter for our freedom from radical slavery calls forth our heart's sincere gratitude.[12]

The most open scandal at the time involved the dishonesty of Judge William Story's federal court of the Western District of Arkansas. According to Col. L.B. Whitney of the Secret Service of Washington, Story claimed expenses for duties never performed, turned loose dangerous criminals, and received numerous bribes as did other officials of the court. Story, in fact, was about to be impeached when he resigned and fled to Denver.[13] Scandals like this had become the exception rather than the rule.

In all this time, from October 1, 1873, until the incident mentioned below, Baxter made not one move that indicated that he was following any course except the one he promised in his campaign —

to make a good governor and to protect the people. Nor was there any sign that he asked any help from either side. He just accepted the help of the people who came to his assistance. He stated to the Poland Committee (page 418) "I have a feeling of independence and not only a disposition but a determination to maintain my own independence and self respect."

The failure of the railroad bond steal bill twelve months before had not affected the original railroad bond bill of July 21, 1868. Approximately $6,200,00 more bonds were eligible to be applied for, and A.H. Johnson, president of the Arkansas Central Railroad, applied for bond aid. The previous fall, this company had failed to sell $500,000 in bonds on American money markets.[14] Senator Stephen Dorsey, who came to Arkansas to manage the railroad, went to Europe to sell the bonds and failed there also. The Arkansas Central was an unpopular railroad because of its narrow gauge of three feet. In desperation, the railroad turned to the state for aid.

On March 16, 1874, Baxter responded to the application by saying he would issue no more bonds because the 1868 Constitution required that all bond issues be approved by the people.[15] Although the enabling act had passed in the 1868 general election, Baxter may have concluded that every individual issue of bonds also had to be approved by the voters. He also indicated that he considered the whole railroad aid act unconstitutional on the grounds that it was adopted by voice vote instead of a roll-call vote. He even admitted that after he became governor he had issued $400,000 of these bonds, of which $300,000 was for the Arkansas Central. However, after re-studying the matter, he decided to issue no more bonds. This announcement brought the radicals into immediate conflict with the governor.

On the day of the announcement, the Little Rock *Republican* reversed its position again and never printed another kind word about Elisha Baxter. The paper soon endorsed Brooks, as did many other radical papers.

The essence of Baxter's reply to Johnson was contained in this passage:

It [the bond aid] fosters corruption and extravagance, and the construction of the roads is forgotten in a struggle of the corporations to secure the public money mainly for private and selfish ends rather than for public benefit.[16]

As usual, Baxter moved without consulting either the Brooks or the Clayton faction.

Senators Clayton and Dorsey came home to Little Rock for a radical conclave to decide what to do about Baxter. One story, denied by Clayton, said he offered Baxter a lucrative federal appointment for his resignation as governor, which would have placed Volney V. Smith in the governor's chair.[17] The governor refused, and Hadley, the go-between, supposedly said:

'Baxter, I have no objection to your politics, but you should let the boys make a little money.' The governor answered: 'What money? The money that was to be wrung from the hard hands of an impoverished people by such measures as the railroad steal bill? The farmers of Arkansas, white and black, women and children, working barefooted, living upon insufficient diet, already plundered to destitution? Yet their scanty stock and stores were to be further taxed to release great corporations from indebtedness, and interest thereon at eight per cent, of millions, and to pay interest on bonds sold to such promoters as Josiah Coldwell, [promoter of Memphis to Fort Smith railroad] in New York and London, for fifty or sixty per cent of their face value, in order that a horde of strangers, without right or merit, should live in vicious indulgence.'[18]

The personal column of the *Republican* and other papers from April 1 to 7 showed a large number of sheriffs and other Republicans from over the state registered at the hotels for the meeting.

According to the conservative *Gazette*, Clayton told Baxter he could no longer support him.[19] The senators quietly went back to Washington, but before leaving they worked out a plan of attack. Clayton allied himself with Brooks, who prepared to take over the governor's position by armed force while Clayton stayed in Washington to influence Grant. Brooks had attacked Grant bitterly in the 1872 campaign and could hardly ask favors.

At the time of this radical conclave, the case of *Brooks* vs. *Baxter* had been in the circuit court of Judge John Whytock of Pulaski County for about ten months. Baxter had filed a demurrer, a case with no legal basis because of the previous decision in the Supreme Court on the *quo warranto* suit. A demurrer requests a dismissal of a suit on the basis that the claim of the plaintiff, even if true, does not represent a criminal offense, is defective, or otherwise insufficient.

Associate Justice Stephenson claimed to the Poland committee[20] that the filing of a demurrer equaled a plea of guilt. Judge Whytock eventually laid the suit aside without any action on it or on the demurrer.

In another case before the Supreme Court in which James R. Berry, who ran on the same ticket with Brooks, tried to displace Wheeler as auditor, the Supreme Court had issued a restraining order to the lower courts ruling that they had no jurisdiction in statewide election contest, which meant that Whytock should have dismissed *Brooks* vs. *Baxter*.

During the last half of 1873, Brooks watched closely for an opportunity to physically attack Baxter, but the Baxter militia had too much strength. Brooks also discovered that his popular support had eroded sharply,[21] but nevertheless he wanted to strike before his influence totally disappeared.

The Poland Committee was so amused at this 180-degree swap in allegience for both sides that the members tried to find the reason. The radicals said it was because of the appointment of Democrats by Baxter. Governor Baxter said that they fell out with him before he appointed a single Democrat, and that it was over the railroad steal bill, Metropolitan Police bill, and the election control bill. The fact that the radicals so quickly and unanimously struck Baxter over these bonds suggests that they owned a lot of them and wanted the state to tax the people and restore them to par.

The reason the radicals took Brooks into their fold was that he still had a good squad of supporters and a law suit in which they could command a decision from a fellow radical judge.

FOOTNOTES

[1] *Arkansas Gazette*, September 21, 1873, 2-2.
[2] *Ibid.*, September 28, 1873, 2-2.
[3] *Ibid.*, October 7, 1873, 1-1, and October 11, 1873, 1-2.
[4] New York *Times*, September 30, 1873, 1-6, and Arkadelphia *Southern Standard*, October 4, 1873, 2-2.
[5] New York *Times*, October 14, 1873, 1-6, and *Arkansas Gazette*, October 10, 11, 1873, 1-2.
[6] *Arkansas Gazette*, August 17, 1874.
[7] New York *Times*, September 20, 1873, 5-4, and Arkadelphia *Southern Standard*, September 27, 1873, 2-3.
[8] *Arkansas Gazette*, February 23, 1873, 1-3.
[9] Arkadelphia *Southern Standard*, October 4, 1873, 2-2.
[10] *Arkansas Gazette*, June 5, 1873, 1-1.
[11] Bassett, p. 635.
[12] *Arkansas Gazette*, September 20, 1873.
[13] New York *Times*, January 12, 1874. 1-2.
[14] *Arkansas Gazette*, October 10, 1873, 1-1.
[15] *Ibid.*, March 20, 1874, and March 21, 1874.
[16] *Ibid.*, March 22, 1874, 2-2.
[17] *Ibid.*, April 8, 1874.
[18] Harrell, p. 197.
[19] *Arkansas Gazette*, March 31, 1874, 1-1.
[20] Poland Report, p. 431.
[21] *Ibid.*, September 2, 1873, 1-2.

Chapter 13

Coup Against A Good Government

With the dismal winter and the March winds behind, April is a pleasant time in Arkansas. In 1874 the people, especially the white conservatives, had a still more pleasant situation: Elisha Baxter's fifteen months in office had crippled the radicals and broken their control of Arkansas. To completely eliminate the radicals, the people, now fully enfranchised and promised a fair election by Baxter, had only to vote out the remainder of the radicals in the fall election.

Only the suit filed by Brooks in the Pulaski County Circuit Court of Judge Whytock remained as a possible threat to Baxter. John Whytock had been appointed judge of this district embracing White and Pulaski Counties by Governor Clayton.

Federal district court began in Little Rock April 15, and Judge Whytock assured E.H. English, Baxter's attorney, who had tried to get the case dismissed the previous Saturday, that he would not consider any cases while federal court was in session.[1] Brooks appeared in court that same day. Judge Whytock then dismissed Baxter's demurrer, granted Brooks his request for the office of governor, and assessed a judgment against Baxter for $2,218, his salary received to date.[2] No records remain of Whytock's judicial reasoning except that he justified deciding the case in the absence of either Baxter or his attorneys on the basis that the case would have to go to the Supreme Court.

The Constitution of 1868 gave the General Assembly the full authority to determine who was elected to state officers and to try contests if the need arose. "Contested elections shall likewise be determined by both houses of the General Assembly in such a manner as it may hereafter be prescribed by law," (Article VI, Section 19). The Constitution provided no appeal to any court.

All decisions of the legislature had been in Baxter's favor, and in the *quo warranto* case, the Arkansas Supreme Court stated:

> Under this Constitution, the determination of the question as to whether a person exercising the office of governor has been duly elected or not, is vested exclusively in the General Assembly of the state, and neither this or any other court has jurisdiction to try a suit in relation to such a contest, be the mode or form what it may, whether at the suit of the Attorney General or the relation of a claimant through him or by an individual alone claiming a right to the office.[3]

With regard to Whytock's decision, the *Gazette* stated: "... the judgment of the circuit court amounts to no more than blank paper."[4]

The *Gazette* later stated, "Baxter, they forced us to take, and Baxter we will force them to keep."[5]

The New York *Times* pronounced Whytock's decision the snap judgment of an inferior court:

> While his opponent was yet ignorant of his designs, he [Brooks] stole upon him with 25 armed men and ejected him from his office. Thereupon, Brooks declared himself to be governor of Arkansas and has been making a great ado about the matter since ... If the higher court had no jurisdiction, it is difficult to imagine how an inferior tribunal obtained it[6]*

Brooks took a copy of the decision and backed by General Catterson of militia fame, and about 25 armed men, including John McClure, Benton Turner, John Booker and other Clayton supporters, presented the decision to Governor Baxter in his office and demanded the governor's retirement.

Baxter was alone except for his young son and a Colonel Howes of St. Francis County, who apparently left without playing any part in the crisis. When Baxter refused to surrender the office, Brooks and his men let him know that they were armed and would eject him by force. Baxter could see more of Brooks's supporters through the door. He left under protest, and his son walked away with him. When the boy reached in his pocket for some tobacco, one of the armed men jabbed him with a gun.[7] Baxter walked about three blocks east to the Anthony House at about 11:30 a.m.

The coup which had been predicted and threatened for a year had come.

The coup forces did not do what they later admitted they considered: taking Baxter prisoner and hiding him somewhere so he could not organize to fight. Such an act would have so outraged the

Arkansas people that bloodshed would probably have been more immediate and serious.

It is striking that about thirty leading radicals could plan and execute such a coup without a leak. Brooks had said that he would be governor or die trying and that if Whytock gave him a decision, he would take the office. That should have been enough warning for Baxter to guard the Capitol day and night. He probably did not realized that two such bitter enemies as Clayton and Brooks were desperate enough to form a combination.

Baxter then went to St. John's Military Academy and placed himself under the protection of Col. O.C. Grey and the cadets. After collecting a number of supporters the next day,[8] he returned to the Anthony House and established headquarters with the cadets acting as his guards. So many prominent Arkansans visited him that night that he knew he was not fighting a lonely battle.

Catterson, who was immediately appointed adjutant general on Brooks's orders, demanded the keys to the state armory from the deputy secretary of state, General Frank Strong (the secretary of state,, James M. Johnson, was out of the state). Strong refused, and on Brooks's orders, doors were broken open and the Capitol fortified with arms in the style of any organized coup.[9]

While Brooks fortified the Capitol, Baxter's friends fortified the Anthony House, about three blocks to the east on Markham Street. Little Rock was soon flooded with excited people, and although men rushed to the aid of both sides, Baxter unquestionably had the greater strength with a preponderance of ex-Confederates. Had federal troops not been present, Baxter could have retaken the Capitol any time, but that would have provoked bloody destruction. Within a week, both sides were fully armed for an intrastate war more serious than any that ever occurred in America.

On the 16th, both contestants wired President Grant. Each one asked for arms, about 1,500 stands, which Baxter had deposited in the federal arsenal. Attorney General George H. Williams made all replies for the President, and denied both contestants the use of the arms and stated that the position of the federal government was only to preserve order and that the courts would have to make the final disposition of the case. Also, on the 16th, Brooks, in a long proclamation to the people promised he would be a good governor.[10] He mentioned that no man had been as badly cheated in politics as he, but Brooks did not tell who had cheated him. It was Powell Clayton and the ring of radicals, and they had taken from him even the lowly jobs in the General Assembly. They were the ones who influenced Grant to remove him, with Catterson and Whipple, from their federal jobs. They were the ones with whom he was then allied. He sprinkled his proclamation with "my rights," "the choice of the people," and "God helping me," and ended with a statement that any attempt to place Baxter back would "lead to bloodshed."[11]

The Brooks force, aided by Clayton, had several days in which to secretly organize, and they were initially stronger than Baxter's force. The Brooks troops at first were primarily blacks.

The first communication from President Grant, sent by Attorney General George Williams, that the courts would decide the matter was encouraging for Brooks, since he controlled the circuit court and the Supreme Court.

The *Republican*, which glorified Baxter for five months to entice him to the radical fold, turned against him the day he refused to issue any more railroad bonds. It treated the Whytock decision of April 15 as a light incident unworthy of notice: "Nothing of importance in the various courts of justice yesterday. An interesting document over the signature of Joseph Brooks, Governor of Arkansas." Then he showed calmly how it wanted the people to behave: "People astonished but did not understand, but facts are facts, and everything done according to law."

Baxter considered himself governor and knew the courts lacked jurisdiction in the conflict. On the 16th, he issued a statement stressing that the reason for the revolt had been his refusal to support fraud in the coming fall election. Baxter was ill, and his wire to Grant said simply, "I propose to take measures immediately to resume possession of the state property and to maintain my authority as the rightful governor of the State."[12] Before the night of the 16th, Baxter declared martial law in Pulaski County.

While Grant's use of troops to prevent bloodshed proved wise, the move first represented aid for Brooks because the challenger could not have lasted long in a contest against such superior numbers.

Immediately after the Brooks coup, Senators Powell Clayton and Stephen Dorsey wired him their blessings, even though Clayton and Brooks had feuded bitterly in the past year. Senators Clayton and Dorsey, and Representatives Hynes, Gause, and Bell, and even the Democratic contender, Gunter, tried to sway Grant to Brooks's cause, but Representative W.W. Wilshire, a conservative Republican, stood by Baxter.[13] Wilshire wired Baxter April 19: "The lawyers in and out of Congress believe you right. Be prompt. Do not fail."

In a meeting on April 17, eighteen Little Rock lawyers signed a statement declaring that Whytock's decision "is one of the more extraordinary acts in judicial history."[14]

It soon became clear that President Grant would eventually

decide the case. On Sunday, April 20, federal troops took position at the north end of Louisiana Street between the two armed forces to prevent a full-scale battle.[15] Each side appointed a number of generals, and the forces grew. According to Pine Bluff authorities, 28-year-old H. King White, a man of considerable fighting ability and experience, agreed with local conservatives to lead the volunteers for Baxter. He apparently admired the way Baxter had stymied the radicals, and brought a large and predominantly black force from Pine Bluff. The others quickly recognized White as the military field general of the Baxter forces. During the Civil War, he had been a member of Morgan's guerrillas, serving in the Indiana raid. Ironically, he had been appointed prosecuting attorney of the Eleventh Judicial Circuit in 1871 by Governor Hadley and had not been reappointed when Baxter took office. Baxter appointed M. McGehee, but White refused to surrender the office and jailed McGehee. Baxter notified White to release McGehee and turn the office over to him or that he, the governor, would see that it was done. He sent the same message to Circuit Judge Morse, and threatened to use the militia if necessary. Thus White learned early to respect Baxter. A commander by nature and experience, White was tall, red and freckled; he became the third man in importance behind Baxter and Brooks in this conflict.

The first company of White's men reached Little Rock on April 19 on the steamboat *Mary Boyd*. The band played and the men sang:
Do you see that boat come round the ben'?
    Goodbye, my lover, goodbye.
She's loaded down with Baxter men,
    Goodbye, my lover, goodbye.
Soon the local poets began to add to this song:
O, for the day that soon shall send
That boat again around the ben,
Goodbye, my lover, goodbye.[16]

On the 20th, 500 additional men came from Pine Bluff on the steamboat *Hallie*. This group consisted mostly of whites.[17] By April 21, White had a sizable army, and Baxter turned back men who were not needed. Brooks's force within the Capitol was variously estimated at from 100 to 150. His force also included a crew inside the nearby Metropolitan Hotel and a number of men scattered around the few blocks that he controlled. Later estimates put his total force at around a thousand.

About 5 p.m. on the 21st, King White marched 300 of his black troops about eight or nine blocks on Scott Street and back on Rock Street to the Anthony House to serenade Baxter. Baxter complimented them but told them that he was too ill to make a speech.

White then asked, "Just tell us whether or not you are going to have us take the Senate House, or not."

"I ask you gentlemen to be patient and quiet," Baxter replied, "conduct yourselves orderly, as good soldiers, such as I know you to be, and in due time proper orders will be given you to assert the rights of the state."[18] He then prepared to retire. White delayed Baxter and told him that contrary to reports, his black troops were loyal and would do their duty and fight, and he added that when the word was given, "In twenty-five minutes Joseph Brooks would be in hell, or the archives . . ."[19]

Due to the cheering of his men, the balance of this remark was not heard by the reporters. White then rode to his troops farther to the west, perhaps to direct them in further activities of the day.

Colonel Rose, commanding the Federal troops, rushed up and asked White if he intended to charge the Capitol. The evidence as to what happened thereafter conflicts, but apparently the horse Rose was riding stumpled into one or two of the musicians. White criticized Rose for this behavior and some observers said Rose then drew his pistol to strike White, and White struck the weapon with his arm and the gun fired into the air.

A black on the sidewalk then shot at Rose. The nervous men responded by indiscriminately firing an estimated 200 shots. David F. Shall, a Little Rock real estate dealer who was standing near a window on the first floor of the Anthony House, was hit in the back and killed.[20] Around ten others were wounded.

Many years later, a son of Baxter, probably quoting his father, said the bullet that killed Shall was probably intended for the governor. Others believed at the time that the killing of Shall was an attempt to assassinate Baxter.[21] During the war, Major Shall was a Confederate cavalry officer under General Hardee. After the war, he became a prominent real estate dealer in Little Rock.

Rose soon brought out fire ladders and equipment and barricaded a line across Markham Street, which became the dividing line between the two forces.

While the real backbone of the Baxter forces was the ex-Confederate people of the state who had opposed him in the election 16 months before, he also had some black support. As the tension mounted, Brooks and Baxter each appointed generals, quartermasters, and lower officers, down to corporals. They observed the rules of war, established battle lines, and posted pickets in various places.

Albert Pike and Robert Ward Johnson were then practicing law in Washington, D.C., and on April 24 they issued a legal interpretation of the issues, which had great influence on the people of the United States. "No inferior court," stated Johnson and Pike, "could overturn the decision of a Supreme Court. The removal of a governor by a state district judge would be just as ridiculous as for any one of a hundred district Federal judges in trying to remove President Grant." On May 1, another legal brief for Baxter was issued by U.M. Rose, joined by Pike, Johnson, and Wilshire. Each of these opinions had great influence in the North.

The attitudes of many people beside these leading lawyers helped the Baxter cause with the President. Grant was then in his second term, and many of his supporters encouraged him to try for a third. He entertained the idea and wanted a solution to the Southern problem. Earlier, the President had refused to send troops to aid the radical contender for the governorship of Texas, and Grant indicated he was tired of dissident radicals running to him for troops. He spoke of a "New Southern Policy" and was grasping for a more conservative profile. Consequently, he hesitated on the Arkansas situation.

On April 20 Brooks formally applied to President Grant for aid to suppress domestic violence. To give validity to the request, a paper signed by Chief Justice McClure and Justices Searle and Stephenson accompanied this wire in which all three men stated that they recognized Brooks as governor.[22]

On the 28th, Governor Baxter wired President Grant requesting him to modify any orders that he had given the troops which would interfere with his reasserting his authority as governor. After the Rose-White affair, the killing of Shall, and the building of the barricade on Markham Street, Baxter wired the President on April 22:

> As I cannot move any troops to assert my claim to the office of governor, without a collision with the United States troops, which I will not bring about under any circumstances, I propose to call the legislature together at an early day, and leave them with the question, as by law they alone have jurisdiction.[23]

He also asked for protection for the members of the legislature in determining a peaceable solution and agreed to abide by the decision. Grant replied:

> I heartily approve any adjustment peaceably, of the pending difficulty in Arkansas, and I will give all assistance and protection I can under the Constitution and laws of the United States, to such modes of adjustment. I hope that the military forces on both sides will now disband.[24]

Baxter gave Grant's message to the members of the General Assembly and called the special meeting for May 11. However, a lot of shooting took place between the time of these messages and May 11. Brooks wrote T. J. Hunt of Fayetteville on April 27 and asked him to cooperate with Judge David Walker and his other friends in Fayetteville in forming a company of armed men to come to Little Rock, "I would like one hundred of your best mountain boys," he asked. He included properly engraved commission forms for appointment of officers. "Come with the boys. I will be glad," and he signed the message, "Governor of Arkansas."[25]

All state officers elected on the same ticket with Baxter were in an identical situation. If Baxter was not elected, they also were not elected. But all of them followed Clayton and supported Brooks, except the Secretary of State, James M. Johnson. Johnson was away when this affair began, but he returned to Little Rock on April 22 and asked Brooks if he could occupy his office. At first, he received the word that he could, but subsequently as Secretary of State he attested to Governor Baxter's call of the legislature.[26] Brooks considered himself to be the governor and regarded Johnson's attestation as one of recognizing the wrong man as governor.

The only other candidate on the Brooks ticket in 1872 who tried to secure office was James R. Berry, who ran for reelection as auditor but was defeated by Stephen Wheeler. Berry was not a carpetbagger but an Arkansas Unionist from Madison County. He had previously been a Democrat but as son-in-law of the former Unionist Governor Isaac Murphy, he supported the Murphy Unionist administration. The courts ruled against Berry's bid to be declared auditor.

The support of the elected officials for Brooks angered Berry, and in a letter to the *Gazette* of around May 1, he expressed his anger for Brooks' acceptance of their aid and stated that the legislature should untangle the mess. This letter placed Berry in Baxter's fold.[27]

On April 30 White and a company of men went south on the steamboat *Hallie* to contest a predominantly black company being organized by Colonel J.W. Murphy, a Pine Bluff politician and supporter of Brooks. White's force surprised and scattered Murphy's men 15 miles east of Pine Bluff at the Cornerstone Church near New Gascony, killing nine men and wounding about twenty. White's company also captured and paroled a large number of the opposition forces. That struggle proved to be the biggest battle of the Brooks-Baxter War, and White, who had only nine men wounded, was thereafter known as the "King of the lower river country."[28]

J.W. Murphy was wounded in the head in this affair. In later years, when someone remarked to King White that Murphy was a self-made man, White answered, "I put a head on him."

Sandwiched among these military activities were some interesting legal developments. Since a circuit court case sparked this revolution, Brooks, acting on behalf of his enemy Baxter, appealed the case to the Supreme Court. But then, unknown parties kidnapped Justices Bennett and Searle and held them incommunicado. Federal troops searched for the judges, but their captors eventually released them after Bennett paid a small sum of money. They then made their way to Brooks's camp in the Capitol. The full court never met, but it did issue an order that the treasurer had authority to issue expense money to Brooks and decided Brooks was the governor.[29] Few people ever paid any attention to this last decision because it was made inside Brooks's military camp. This kidnapping incident failed to help the Baxter cause even though no one has ever claimed that the governor was personally connected with the affair. It was apparently a kidnapping for ransom.

At 3 a.m. May 8, the steamboat *Hallie*,[30] carrying Baxter troops under Captain Sam Houston, started up the Arkansas River to intercept a flatboat bringing to the Brooks camp 160 stands of arms and ammunition taken without authority from the Arkansas Industrial University of Fayetteville. The Brooks force sent a larger company under John Brooker by railroad, and they encamped on the steep bank of the Arkansas River where the river narrowed and received the waters of Palarm Creek.[31]

Fighting began between the men on the boat and those on land. Captain Houston was killed and several of his men were wounded, one of which later died. Two of the Brooks men were also killed. A bullet pierced a steam pipe on the *Hallie* and disabled the boat. The *Hallie* then flated downstream and lodged against the bank on the south side where the Brooks forces captured the disabled vessel. However, the Baxter men retreated to their camp in Little Rock,[32] having failed to prevent the guns from reaching Brooks.

A number of individual casualties occurred in skirmishes throughout the state. Companies of men marched around Little Rock and back to their permanent locations as they would in any military conflict. The presence of the federal troops kept the main army of each faction from attacking the other side, although the minor incidents increased. Many people feared that more fighting would break out over the state.

On Sunday, May 10, Dr. Weldon E. Wright made $20,000 available to Baxter and said that $200,000 or all he had would also be made available. Like Wright, many of the old substantial citizens had decided that Brooks must go.[33]

On the same day, Brooks dispatched some troops to the rail terminals in Argenta to prevent reinforcements from reaching

Baxter. King White defeated them and wounded several of Brooks' men before Rose brought federal troops across the river to stop the fight.

On May 12, Brooks again sent troops north about ten blocks to near the railroad station to prevent the landing of Baxter reinforcements sent by boat from the western part of the state. Soon Baxter men, who were sent to the penitentiary grounds (now the State House grounds) attacked the Brooks force. Both sides sent reinforcements which included about all the men Brooks had at his disposal. This battle would have resulted in a major fight with heavy casualties on both sides as well as possible civilian losses had not Rose again marched federal troops between them.

As the tension mounted, William Woodruff, Jr., secured some guns from Galveston and trained them on the Capitol. The big 64-pounder now mounted on the old Capitol grounds and named "Lady Baxter" was dug half out of the ground at the foot of Byrd Street and repaired. The ladies of Little Rock wreathed these guns with flowers and furnished Baxter's troops with excellent food. Brooks' situation was deteriorating fast with many of his men going over to Baxter's side.

A number of messages had gone to Washington and replies received which were not entirely pertinent to the final decision, but since the General Assembly was to meet on May 11, Grant wired Baxter on that date:

> I recommend that the membership of the General Assembly, now in Little Rock, adjourn for a reasonable time, say for ten days, to enable Brooks to call into the body his supposed adherents... Brooks' friends here agree that if this course is pursued no opposition will be made to the meeting of the Assembly in the State-house as usual, and that he will do the same. I urgently request that all armed forces on both sides be dismissed so that the General Assembly may act free from any military pressures...

Baxter replied immediately that until a quorum was present the General Assembly had the authority only to adjourn from day to day and that he had no objections to their doing so, and after a quorum met, they could adjourn until the Brooks supporters arrived. He would dismiss his troops in proportion to Brooks' dismissal of his. Baxter proposed that Brooks leave the Capitol and remain as far west of it as Baxter was east, deposit the state arms in the Armory, and turn over all state buildings "to the secretary of state to whom under the law they belong." Forty-six members of the General Assembly endorsed this message.[34] This marked the beginning of the end for Brooks, for he could now realize that the problem was finally in the hands of the authority provided by the constitution of 1868 (which he helped write) to handle contested elections of state officers.

U.S. Attorney General Williams replied that the President considered this proposition reasonable and had asked Brooks to accept it. Throughout this crisis, Williams advised Grant on a policy that favored Baxter. After reviewing the *quo warranto* decision of 1873, Williams saw that Whytock's decision ran contrary to it and that the General Assembly would have to decide the issue,[35] and the General Assembly was then pro Baxter.

The New York *Times* on May 13 became discouraged by the continuation of the fight, then in its fourth week:

We look upon this state of affairs as one of the most disgraceful occurrences in the history of this country... Can it be held that any state in the Union has the right to carry on a civil war to determine which of two claimants were lawfully elected its governor? A dispute of that kind might be going on in several states at once — in Texas, in South Carolina, in New York — and the Federal Congress is to look on unconcerned while perhaps half the country is at war?... arises in some degree from the reconstruction policy pursued by Congress.

Brooks realized that according to law the General Assembly (then mostly men elected after the Confederates were enfranchised) had the authority to decide the issue. In order to keep a decision out of the legislature, he made one last desperate effort — he sent a long telegram to President Grant, quoted in part:

If you have the power under the Constitution and laws of the United States to settle the question of who is Governor of Arkansas, adverse to the decisions of the courts of the state, settle it, and settle it at once. I shall not resist what you may order your troops to do, but shall with all the force at my command repel any and all attempts of Baxter's forces to take possession of the state house.

But the New York *Times* of May 13 noted that "the dispatches from Brooks are so defiant and almost impudent in tone toward the Federal authority, that little hope is left of effecting anything by compromise."

Brooks then sent a 400-word, ill-tempered message to Williams which, combined with the one to Grant, sealed his fate. The note said that even if a quorum was present, it did not constitute a legislature because it had not been called by a governor (only by Baxter who, he claimed, was not a governor). Brooks said he would not disband any troops until the question of the rightful governor was settled or until he was required to do so by the President. The other side, he said, had fired on federal troops, plundered and robbed and "commenced indiscriminate slaughter of colored men" (apparently referring to the fight at Cornerstone). Grant was shocked at Brooks' crude attitude in lecturing to him about his duties and took his time in answering.

Only 17 answered roll call in the House on May 11, but there were 36 on the 12th. A quorum of 45 arrived on the 13th,[36] and a quorum met in the Senate on the following day. Even though some of the Brooks supporters had not arrived, the legislature's organization was completed, and Baxter delivered his message on the 14th.[37]

Some of the Brooks men failed to attend because they recognized that they were losing strength and that the meeting place in Ditter Block lay within the Baxter lines. However, those Brooks men who did show up met no opposition from the Baxter supporters. Volney V. Smith, lieutenant governor and a Brooks supporter, served as President of the Senate, and the other Brooks men who attended voted and spoke as they pleased with few reservations. Old officers who did not attend were replaced by newly elected officers: Senator Frierson as president pro tem of the Senate, and James H. Berry as Speaker of the House; both men were Baxter supporters.[38]

Brooks wanted the courts to decide the dispute because he knew that while Clayton no longer controlled the General Assembly, he had the Supreme Court in his charge. In fact, three members of the Court had wired Grant that they considered Brooks to be the lawful governor.

The President then made his decision, as Brooks requested, and the first that Brooks knew of it was when Grant's telegram of May 15 to the newly-elected officers of the General Assembly was read at the Anthony House.[39] The cheering lasted for thirty minutes, and the hearts of the Brooks men sank when they heard the news. The lengthy message recognized Baxter as governor and directed him to keep the peace as requested by the legislature. Grant commanded the insurgents to disband and asked the military authorities of both sides to cooperate in furnishing transportation for both groups to their homes.[40]

While Governor Baxter had already hobbled the radical government in Arkansas, Grant's message ended the radicals' last hope for even a small share of the government. The conservatives outnumbered the radicals by at least two to one and at least had possession of the government.

Along with Baxter, U.S. Attorney General George H. Williams played an important role in the downfall of the Brooks rebellion. As U.S. Senator from Oregon before entering Grant's cabinet, Williams had been an active moderate Republican. Before Grant sent his final telegram recognizing Baxter as governor, he asked Williams for a legal opinion on the situation and Williams' opinion clearly favored Baxter.

Several days before Williams gave Grant the opinion, Brooks had tried to get the Whytock decision before the Arkansas Supreme Court, ensconced within his fortified Capitol. State Treasurer Page rejected Brooks' warrant for $1,000 for expenses, stating that "Brooks was not governor." Brooks then applied for a mandamus to force Page to honor his warrant. The Court obliged by stating that Whytock's decision was proper and declaring Brooks the governor. Williams told Grant about this clandestine scheme and mentioned that Page had previously paid some of Brooks' expenses.[41]

However, the about-face the Court made in light of its previous *quo warranto* decisions brought the strongest rebuke from Williams:

> It is not too much to say that it presents a case of judicial insubordination which deserves the reprobation of everyone who does not wish to see public confidence in the certainty and good faith of judicial proceedings wholly destroyed.[42]

Despite Williams' opinion, among the leading state and congressional officials only James M. Johnson, Secretary of State and U.S. Representative W.W. Wilshire supported Baxter.[43] The balance had radical backgrounds or had been elected by the radical machine and supported Brooks.

The New York *Times* summarized the events by commenting on Grant's message:

> The effect of the President's decision will probably be to break up the powerful corrupt machine. Clayton and Dorsey are in rage, breathing forth threats. The entire delegation from Arkansas, except Wilshire, wanted courts to decide. The popular belief as to the change is that Arkansas had been in the clutches of a corrupt machine.
>
> Crowds of men, women, and children now crowd the streets, stores reopening, flags waving, and bands playing. Trains began running to Memphis.
>
> The actions of Judge Whytock in the face of the Berry-Wheeler case is little more than judicial insubordination.[44]

Within a day, many radicals fled by horses or by train without anyone trying to prevent their flight, and for days no one knew where they had gone. Even Speaker of the House C.W. Tankersley hid in a baggage car and took abut $53,000 railroad bond money with him.

The cleanup crew found everything in the Capitol in disarray. Several hundred men had tried to live for a month in and around the small building. The *Gazette* of May 20 described the conditions:

"The building was filthy; a mixed perfume of sour bacon and human being pervaded the entire edifice with a nauseating ordor. Furniture had been moved around for barricades. Guns lay around everywhere. State books had been trampled on and some ruined."

By late afternoon of the 19th, officials notified Baxter that things were ready for his occupancy. The cannons, including the Lady Baxter, were fired in salute to the occasion.[45] Citizens held meetings all over Little Rock to celebrate the victory, and throughout the state barbecues and parties saluted Baxter's victory. The governor's office was illuminated for the night, and Baxter remained late to receive callers and well wishers.

Telegrams poured in to congratulate the governor. A typical one from Pine Bluff read:

> God Bless Baxter, You and Yours,
> Sing, Brother, Sing.
> B.S. Williams[46]

Two thousand men marched through Little Rock in Baxter's victory parade, and Brooks' men stood along the sideline dumbfounded at Baxter's support. Baxter's triumph clearly marked the destruction of Clayton's machine.

More men were killed in this conflict than were listed in the three battles — Cornerstone, Palarm, and Markham Street. Scattered killings over the state occurred and authorities estimated that perhaps 200 lives were lost.[47] Whether or not this estimate is high as this study indicates is hard to determine today. However, if federal troops had not been present, many more would have lost their lives, and the Capitol and other buildings might have been destroyed. About 2,000 came to Baxter's aid, and probably 1,000 to Brooks', and both sides were fully determined to fight the contest to a bloody finish.[48] Brooks held a defensive position with breastworks, and Rose defended him from attack. The Adjutant General estimated the financial loss in the conflict at $250,000.[49]

Clayton wrote in his memoirs[50] that Baxter's successful recapture of the state government was one of the most disgraceful incidents ever to take place in American politics. However, Baxter's actions speeded the return of Arkansas to normal government by four years, because in the early spring of 1877 President Rutherford B. Hayes withdrew federal troops from the South and allowed the Southern conservatives to expel the remaining radical governments.

This was exactly four years from the time when Baxter aided in the defeat of the railroad steal bill and Clayton lost control of Arkansas.

That everybody considered the Brooks Revolution to be a small war is shown by the fact that when peace occurred, no official accusations of murder or any other crime were made against any of the participants. On May 27, the General Assembly, happy to see the end of the "war," considered a resolution of pardon and amnesty of all who had taken part in the rebellion. The legislature initially excluded Brooks from the pardon, but on reflection and a request by J.H. Berry, he was included.[51]

Although most radical leaders fled,[52] many returned because of the conciliatory attitude of the conservatives. Messages went to the North from the pens of radicals that a victory for Baxter would mean the wholesale slaughter of the radicals and blacks, but of course this did not occur, and soon many of Brooks' leaders, such as Catterson, Whipple, and Rice, were seen on the streets of Little Rock.[53]

Before the leading followers of Brooks like McClure and Upham had returned to their Little Rock homes from the Capitol, Baxter ordered their houses guarded to prevent violence by any of his more lawless followers. The guards reported that they were taken in by the wives, who provided well for them.

The 88 Fort Smith troops who supported Brooks marched to their steamer, *Robert Semple*, under a peace agreement and embarked for home, happy and singing.

Governor Baxter proclaimed:

Finally, let us together give thanks to the great God of armies who has blessed our cause. Let us remember with great gratitude the great citizen soldier, the President of the United States, who has at length seen the justice of our cause ... Let not our friends, the people, have any cause to censure you for any disorder or riotous conduct in the moment of victory.[54]

The General Assembly passed a joint resolution of thanks to Grant which also said, "That the struggle had not been between Northern and Southern, not between Republicans and Democrats, but, without political affiliations, between good government and bad."[55] It also asked people of the North, South, East and West to come to Arkansas and help build the state.[56]

As for the extent of this revolution, none other in American history equals this Brooks coup or revolution. Two centuries before, Bacon's rebellion occurred in Virginia against Governor Berkley, who was appointed by King Charles II. Many of Bacon's men died fighting the Indians, and many were executed by Berkley after Bacon died. However, it did not equal the later conflict in Arkansas. In 1842, Thomas Darr organized an armed revolt against the government of Rhode Island which resulted in needed constitutional reforms, but no armed conflict took place. The Whiskey Rebellion in Pennsylvania in 1794 was small by comparison. Nothing within any American state has equaled the Brooks rebellion and no other conflict resulted in such a complete change of leadership.

While this queer contest was in full swing, the New York *Herald*, being confused at the shifts in position which both Baxter and Brooks had taken, asked Baxter for an explanation. The statement in the *Times* was a review of the past except it affirmed that the radicals offered Baxter a federal judgeship and all the money he wanted for his resignation. The position offered Baxter was the Western District of Arkansas and Indian Territory, which was later given to the famous Judge Isaac Parker.

In his message to the General Assembly May 23, Baxter asked for the payment of the expenses of putting down the rebellion.[57]

In this administration, Baxter turned completely against the ones who elected him governor. That change probably first occurred as he traveled with Clayton and observed his behavior in the 1872 campaign. When Clayton and Hynes were calling each other liars and thieves at Oliver Springs, Baxter, according to Harrell, just smiled as if he considered the source and made his common speech for honest government.[58]

Many observers at the time and several later commentators have charged the Elisha Baxter government with being too lenient with those who took part in the rebellion. However, several factors should be considered. First, Baxter was essentially a peaceable man. He and the legislators also had a precedent in the recent Civil War in that only one man, Henry Wirz, the officer in charge of the Andersonville Prison camp, was executed as a war criminal. Everyone else, except Jefferson Davis, eventually received their pardon and amnesty. The U.S. policy and the Baxter policy proved about the same — no criminal prosecution.[59]

On the other hand, the Baxter forces did impose a political penalty. The House of Representatives in the special session on May 25 received from its Judiciary Committee a bill of impeachment against John McClure, Chief Justice of the Supreme Court, associate justices John E. Bennett, Elhanan J. Searle, and Marshall L. Stephenson; Stephen Wheeler, auditor; William H. Gray, commissioner of emigration; and nine other county and district officers. Governor Baxter recommended the impeachment of all who took part in the rebellion.[60] While this was going on, Clayton and Dorsey remained defiant and wired Brooks that Congress would investigate, with favorable results.[61]

The House impeached McClure, Wheeler, Searle, Bennett, Gray, and some lower officers with only a few dissenting votes. Due to the predetermined adjournment on May 28, the impeachment of others and the trials in the Senate for those already impeached had to be set for the December session of the General Assembly.[62] However, many radical officeholders simply resigned and left the state, including the then-famous Judge Whytock. This study has never found a trace of Whytock and several others after this date. William Henry Harrison Clayton, judge of the Fifth Judicial Circuit and Powell Clayton's brother, also resigned.[63] A news item in the St. Louis *Republican* reported that Searle, Upham, Barbour and Benton Turner had arrived there.[64] Some radicals went to Washington, D.C. to beg federal help, some went north and others went west. President Grant gave federal jobs to most of those who went west, and those who stayed in Arkansas became postmasters or deputies under the federal courts.

Only Upham was arrested for his militia crimes for the murder of Thorpe. Since nobody could be produced, however, prosecution was abandoned.

A few days after the special session of the General Assembly on May 11, 1874, began, General R.C. Newton, commander-in-chief of the Baxter forces, criticized the General Assembly for allowing John M. Clayton and General L.L. Thompson, who had taken part in the rebellion, to take their legislative seats, and his letter was addressed to the soldiers of the state militia.[65] Governor Baxter promptly wrote the legislature that the criticism was made without his consent or approval, for Grant had required that those opposed to Baxter be allowed to keep their legislative seats.[66] Newton immediately resigned his commission. Governor Baxter wrote Newton an explanation in courteous terms but did not retreat from his firm position. He then appointed Newton state treasurer to replace Henry Page, a Brooks man who had resigned.[67] Newton, however, was a well-respected person whose father, Thomas W. Newton, was the only Whig ever to serve in Congress from Arkansas. R.C. lived in Little Rock and practiced law for many years.

Overall, Baxter's lenient policy of dealing with the radicals went a long way toward healing the wounds of the Reconstruction era in Arkansas.

FOOTNOTES

[1] Harrell, p. 188.
[2] *Ibid.*, p. 202.
[3] *Arkansas Supreme Court Reports*, 1873, p. 139.
[4] *Arkansas Gazette*, April 16, 1874, 1-1.
[5] *Ibid.*, April 16, 1874, 1-2.

⁶ New York *Times*, April 20, 1874, 4-3.

* Anyone today wishing to research this matter and not wanting to use Arkansas papers could select no better paper than the New York *Times* (Republican) for it carried a daily heading of "Arkansas."

⁷ Memo from the bar of Independence County upon the death of Elisha Baxter.

⁸ Harrell, p. 206.

⁹ *Arkansas Gazette*, April 16, 1874, 4-3, and Arkadelphia *Southern Standard*, May 18, 1874, 2-6.

¹⁰ Arkadelphia *Southern Standard*, April 18, 1874, 2-6.

¹¹ *Arkansas Gazette*, April 17, 1874, 4-5.

¹² Harrell, p. 208.

¹³ New York *Times*, April 20, 1874, 4-3.

¹⁴ *Arkansas Gazette*, April 18, 1874, 1-1.

¹⁵ Little Rock *Republican*, April 20, 1874.

¹⁶ Harrell, p. 220.

¹⁷ *Arkansas Gazette*, April 21, 1874, 4-4, and Harrell, pp. 219-20.

¹⁸ *Ibid.*, p. 225.

¹⁹ *Arkansas Gazette*, April 22, 1874, 5-3.

²⁰ Harrell, p. 229

²¹ New York *Times*, April 22, 1874, 4-1.

²² New York *Times*, May 16, 1874, 1-2.

²³ *Journal of House of Representatives of Arkansas*, 1874, p. 1.

²⁴ *Ibid.*, p. 2, and Harrell, p. 231.

²⁵ Original letter in files of Washington County Historical Society, Fayetteville, Arkansas.

²⁶ *Arkansas Gazette*, May 24, 1874, 4-3.

²⁷ *Ibid.*, May 2, 1874, 1-5, and Harrell, p. 238.

²⁸ *Arkansas Gazette*, May 1, 1874, 1-1.

²⁹ *Ibid.*, May 7, 1874, 4-3, and May 8, 1874, 1-3.

³⁰ Fayetteville *Democrat*, May 16, 1874.

³¹ Little Rock *Republican*, May 9, 1874, and *Arkansas Gazette*, May 9, 1874, 4-3.

³² New York *Times*, May 9, 1974, 1-2.

³³ James H. Atkinson, *Arkansas Historical Review*, Vol. 4, p. 140; Fletcher, pp. 259-60.

³⁴ New York *Times*, May 12, 1874, 1-2.

³⁵ *Arkansas Gazette*, May 14, 1874, and May 15, 1874, 1-1.

³⁶ Arkadelphia *Southern Standard*, April 15, 1874, 2-2.

³⁷ *Journal of the General Assembly*, pp. 1 and 2.

³⁸ Little Rock *Republican*, May 18-19, 1874.

³⁹ *Arkansas Gazette*, May 16, 1874.

⁴⁰ New York *Times*, May 16, 1874, 1-1.

⁴¹ *Arkansas Gazette*, May 16, 1874, 4-3.

⁴² *Arkansas Supreme Court Reports*, #29, pp. 173-202.

⁴³ *Arkansas Gazette*, May 17, 1874, 1-1.

⁴⁴ New York *Times*, May 16, 1874, 1-2.

⁴⁵ *Ibid.*, May 20, 1874, 5-3.

⁴⁶ *Ibid.*, May 20, 1874, 5-3.

⁴⁷ Thomas Staples, *Reconstruction in Arkansas*, (New York: Columbia University Press, 1924), p. 241.

⁴⁸ *Arkansas Gazette*, May 19, 1874, 2-3.

⁴⁹ *Journal of the Arkansas House of Representatives*, 1874, p. 207.

⁵⁰ Powell Clayton, *Aftermath of the Civil War*, (New York: The Meade Publishing Company, 1914), p. 345.

[51] Little Rock *Republican*, May 27, 1874, 4-2.
[52] *Arkansas Gazette*, May 14, 1874, 4-3.
[53] New York *Times*, May 18, 1874, 5-3.
[54] New York *Times*, May 18, 1874, 5-3.
[55] *Arkansas Gazette*, May 23, 1874, 1-3.
[56] *Acts of General Assembly of State of Arkansas, Special Session, 1874*, Joint Resolution No. VII, p. 54.
[57] *Arkansas Gazette*, May 24, 1874.
[58] Harrell, p. 144.
[59] *Arkansas Gazette*, May 21, 1874, 1-4.
[60] *Ibid.*, May 24, 1874, 1-3.
[61] New York *Times*, May 19, 1874, 1-3.
[62] *Journal of the Arkansas House of Representatives, 1874*, pp. 258-72. Little Rock *Republican*, May 26, 1874, 4-2, 3, 4, 5, 6.
[63] *Arkansas Gazette*, May 24, 1874.
[64] *Ibid.*, May 22, 1874, 2-1.
[65] *Journal of the Arkansas House of Representatives, 1874*, May 20, p. 113.
[66] *Arkansas Gazette*, May 21, 1874, 1-2.
[67] Little Rock *Republican*, May 21-22, pp. 43-44.

Chapter 14

The Father of Arkansas

Elisha Baxter is the only governor in the history of Arkansas who officiated in determining the end of his career. Before the armed rebellion began, Baxter had begun to call for a new constitution to replace the radical Constitution of 1868.[1] In particular, Arkansas needed a document that would end the vast appointive powers of the governor and end the voter registration system with its sweeping powers granted to the governor.

For a great part of Baxter's 22 months as governor, he had stood alone. The radicals who elected him soon turned against him as a traitor to their cause. Some Democrats disliked him because he was a Republican. Some ex-Confederates disliked him because he first refused to fight for the Confederacy, and, after his escape from prison, fought for the Union. While he enjoyed immediate popularity in 1874 and could have been reelected governor, he knew that if he remained in politics, this enmity would arise again. In addition, he was ill. He considered running but only if Joseph Brooks opposed him. Then, too, any political ambitions might create the impression that his previous actions had been purely political strategy for future political rewards.

In the special session which Baxter called for May 11, 1874, to end the Brooks rebellion, as people referred to the event at the time, the governor recommended an election on whether to call a constitutional convention and to elect delegates if the convention carried.[2] This request was granted in Act 2 of that same assembly. The election was held June 30, 1874, and, even though it was opposed by Brooks, Clayton, and other radicals, the convention carried overwhelmingly by a vote of 80,259 to 8,607, passing in every county except Jefferson, Chicot, and Perry. Seventy-three of the 90 delegates elected were conservatives and only 12 were radical.[3]

The very first act of this General Assembly of 1874 was to give substantial extension of time for the redemption of land delinquent for the 1872 and 1873 taxes. Many Arkansas people lost their land because of heavy taxes in the previous administrations, which caused the legislators to give the matter first priority.

The constitution convention began July 14.[4] Grandison D. Royston of Hempstead County, the only delegate who was a member of the first constitutional convention of 1836, was elected president, and Thomas W. Newton was elected secretary. Elisha Baxter and James M. Johnson, the only executive officer who stood by Baxter in the Brooks rebellion, were invited to the Convention. Augustus H. Garland and E.H. English were most influential in helping write the new constitution, and the old Unionist Governor Isaac Murphy supported it.[5] The Constitution of 1874 was soon framed, and became the constitution which Arkansas has used since that year.

The Convention adjourned August 9, and the constitution which had been formed called for an election of new officers from the governor down to the justices of the peace. The new document stripped the governor of his vast appointive powers and greatly limited the taxing power of the state, the counties, and the cities, and reduced the terms of the governor and other state officers from four to two years. Baxter told the Poland Committee that he wished that the appointive power would be taken from him and from his successors, and much of it was removed in this constitution.

On September 8, the day before the Constitutional Convention ended,[6] the Democratic party convention began. A majority of the Democratic county conventions over the state sent delegates pledged to Baxter. Even though many uncompromising Democratic politicians opposed Baxter because he had been a Whig in the beginning, a Democrat after the Whig Party died, and a Republican after the war, a great majority of the delegates favored him, and nominated him by a vote of 52 to 20.[7] No doubt this put a strain on Baxter. He was sitting as a visitor in the convention of the opposition party. Yet, in 18 months he had completely whipped and expelled the radicals from Arkansas politics, but Baxter feared that acceptance of the Democratic nomination would cause people to think that the drastic actions he had taken were done to establish his position in the ascending party, and a true understanding of his actions by the people was more important to him than another term as governor.

Several Democratic delegates defended Baxter from attack on his Republican affiliation. Augustus Garland said, "He was not for men, but for principles." H. King White said, "If George Washington is entitled to be called the father of his country, Elisha

Baxter is entitled to be called the father of Arkansas."

Baxter, however, held fast to his decision and replied by letter: During the period that I have held the office of governor, I have had no alternative except either to actively assist in the destruction of the last vestiges of the liberties of the people, or else to make a stand at all hazards in defense of their rights. I claim no credit for my having pursued the plain path of duty so vital to the public welfare. In doing so, I have violated no pledge. The platform on which I ran was made up of promises for better government ... I have forfeited no pledge, have violated no promise thus made.[8]

The convention moved that Baxter be nominated unanimously, and the measure carried without a dissenting vote. Baxter refused again, saying that he had nothing to add to his previous statement.[9] He then reminisced of representatives who were strangers to the people they represented, and of the bad government resulting, and that it was not possible for such conditions to long continue.

Perhaps no other officeholder has ever received the unanimous vote of the nomination convention of the opposite party for its highest office.

Baxter took practically no part in politics after leaving office. Some newspaper editorials in 1876 speculated that he wanted to be U.S. Senator, but he made no announcement to that effect. Apparently in answer to an inquiry from John M. Harrell in that year, he stated definitely that he did not wish to be governor and authorized publication of his letter.

Candidates for all offices were then nominated by the party conventions and elected by the people in the general election except the U.S. Senators, who were elected by the joint houses of the General Assembly. In short, the party machines picked the U.S. Senators. Baxter belonged to the Republican Party still controlled by Powell Clayton.

Baxter remained a hero to Arkansans of all parties. He came to the Metropolitan Hotel in Little Rock on June 29, 1876, and an immense crowd of citizens and the Rose City Band came to serenade him. He spoke and admitted he was a Republican but complimented the Democrats for what they had done for the state. This proved to be his final goodbye to Arkansas politics.

Baxter retired to Batesville for twenty-five years of service as a practicing attorney. His son, Dr. E.A. Baxter, served as a respected doctor in adjoining Izard County.[10] His grandchildren attended the University of Arkansas along with the grandchildren of Joseph Brooks, and when they met, it was always on a friendly basis. Dr.

Baxter's grandson, Dr. Baxter Billingsley, is now assistant professor of history at South Florida University in Tampa, Florida.[11]

One of the most glowing tributes to Baxter came from Tennessee soon after the Brooks rebellion. The *Memphis Appeal* wrote:

> Every democrat and conservative throughout this broad union, rejoices at the triumph of Governor Elisha Baxter, of Arkansas, over Clayton and his minions . . . for thus standing nobly erect in the hour of greatest need and sorest trial, bearing the brunt of the battle, he deserves, and is receiving, the thanks of every generous and grateful heart. His firmness, endurance and ability has made him the idol of the people. Truly is he worthy of the love and gratitude which gushes from generous hearts, not only in Arkansas, but from one end of the union to the other.
>
> He has labored to shield his people from the dark, murky cloud of corruption that was muttering and gathering for their destruction. The ship of state was fast drifting toward the vortex of ruin, and with cool and dauntless courage he piloted it out of danger. A few weeks since everything was dark and cheerless in Arkansas; but through the pluck and ironhearted courage of Gov. Baxter, the shaded orb of the state breaks through the dark shadows, and prosperity and tranquility belted in one bright bow spans the redeemed and regenerated commonwealth. All praise to Elisha Baxter. In the name of the people of Memphis, we thank him; and in doing so we echo the Voice of Tennessee . . .[12]

H. King White's career after the coup remained significant but not in state political affairs. He wanted to run for U.S. Representative in 1874 but received no support from the Democratic leaders. He then returned to Pine Bluff for life.

On June 10, 1874, nearly 60 days after the collapse of the radical regime, Robert Derry, an employee of John M. Clayton, and several other political radicals attacked White on Barraque Street in Pine Bluff. White was slightly wounded, but Derry, after firing his gun, ran into a store. White dropped to the ground and shot Derry through the window. Several radicals who were with Derry were indicted but apparently nothing was done to them.

In 1879 White served one term in the state Senate from Jefferson County. He served seven terms as mayor of Pine Bluff and had done a lot to clean up the town, promoting better water and sewer systems, improved streets, and law and order. During his tenure in Pine Bluff, it grew from a river port of 1,500 to a city of 20,000. White became an outstanding speaker and a much sought-after defense attorney in serious criminal cases, even those far from Jefferson County.

White died in Pine Bluff January 10, 1907. Upon his death the press credited him with great popularity with poor people. The Pine Bluff *Commercial* stated that his goodness of heart was his greatest fault and that he divided his money with those in need.

In this 1874 convention the Democrats nominated Augustus H. Garland for governor, Elbert H. English for chief justice of the Supreme Court, and David Walker and William M. Harrison for associate justices. James M. Johnson, another Republican who had supported Baxter in the destruction of the Clayton machine, was considered for secretary of state, but Johnson, like Baxter, had his name withdrawn.[13]

On September 11, a day after Johnson declined the convention's nomination for secretary of state, the *Gazette*, which had bitterly criticized Johnson in 1871 for helping make the trade which sent Powell Clayton to the U.S. Senate, published the following statement:

> James M. Johnson; Having ourselves contributed perhaps more than any other influence, under a mistaken apprehension of the facts, to attach undeserved stigma to the political fame of ex-Lieutenant Governor James M. Johnson, we now without solicitation, take the opportunity now presented by the inauguration of a new era of good will, to assert publicly what we have done impliedly for more than two years past, to-wit: Our full belief that in all the trials of the difficult position he has held for the past three years, he has been actuated solely by the desire to emancipate his people at the earliest possible moment in which it could be successfully done. Such was our belief in 1872, and such it is today. His role has been a most difficult one. A less earnest and honorable man would have failed. He has contributed as much as any man in Arkansas to bring about the good time now at hand.

Johnson also had been a Whig, a Unionist, and a Republican, and he decided not to change his political allegiance again. A physician, Johnson's only subsequent governmental position was examiner of Union veterans to see if their disabilities justified pensions. He died at his home near Wesley in Madison County in 1913. He was always known as "Colonel Johnson," and his gravestone, a few hundred feet from his log house, is marked simply "Colonel James M. Johnson."

While the press properly called the Brooks-Baxter struggle a revolution, James M. Harrell wrote one of the first narratives of that tragedy entitled *The Brooks-Baxter War*. History will probably always so designate the affair as did Harrell, but the Brooks Revolution or the Radical Revolution is more appropriate.

After this struggle, the Democratic party wisely bid for the conservative people — Democrats or Republicans - to come into their party. The Republicans, still under the Clayton influence, did not invite them — a fatal blunder. While true republicanism and true radicalism were different political forces, the failure of Clayton and his followers to embrace the conservatives relegated the Republican Party to a minor role in Arkansas for a century.

During these times, men often switched parties, not knowing where they could best serve Arkansas or themselves. For example, W.W. Wilshire, who lost his Republican position in Congress for supporting Baxter, was elected to the same position as a Democrat. The Democrats called back to their fold those who had been Unionist during the War or supported Brooks in the rebellion. The failure of the radicals who were then strong in the Republican Party to do the same, relegated the party to a hopelessly minor position in Arkansas.

As a reflection of Democratic ascendancy, the constitution was adopted on October 13, 1874 by a vote of 78,697 to 24,867, and since the Republicans delined to name a ticket, Democrats were elected to all state offices.[14]

The Republicans held their convention beginning September 15, but it became a convention of defeat and hate. It was sprinkled with such names as Powell Clayton, R.F. Catterson, W.H. Gray, John McClure, John M. Clayton, Judge Searle, Stephen Wheeler, J.N. Sarber, Volney V. Smith, and Stephen Dorsey, and not one lived in Arkansas prior to 1865. Powell Clayton on the evening of September 16 did not take his recent defeat with good humor:

> Elisha Baxter and Gus Garland have by their criminal embraces, brought forth a child in swaddling clothes. It was born from adultery and has written across its forehead — 'bastard.' It will not live long, it will soon be put under ground. You won't weep much.

He defended his gubernatorial administration by telling how he squelched the K.K.K. with his militia. He condemned by name many of the men who had aided in the execution of his political machine. Justice McClure, who had resigned after he was impeached, contended that everything done after Judge Whytock ruled against Baxter was illegal, including the new constitution.

The radicals were not yet willing to give up their lucrative positions. By the fall of 1874, they were out of office and short of cash. A letter was published and signed by D.P. Upham of militia fame, former Justice Searle, Benton Turner of railroad steal bill fame, and others, asking each of their supporters to send them twenty dollars. The money was to be used to send a delegation (probably the ones who signed the letter) to Washington to work for the overturn of the Constitution of 1874 and to reestablish the 1868 Constitution. No one knows what response they received.

Those in Congress who felt dissatisfied with the destruction of the radical government of Arkansas provided for a committee under Representative Luke Poland of Vermont to investigate the entire situation. In early June, 1874, the committee questioned the Arkansas delegation in Congress and those radicals who had fled from Arkansas to Washington. Then the committee decided to finish the investigation at Little Rock, the scene of the strife.

While few opinions were changed, the report of over 500 pages of small type is a good supplement to the press reports of that day and is fairly essential to a full understanding of this attempted coup. Having lost the struggle, the radicals supported the investigation and furnished a large group of nondescript witnesses who charged Baxter with committing fraud. One N.L. Hill forgot that his friends wanted to prove that Baxter stole the 1872 election, and when asked, "who ran that campaign?" proudly stated, "Senator Clayton." Subesequently, Mr. Hill admitted that he supported Baxter, but as governor, Baxter refused him $10,000 from his emergency fund to establish a pro-Baxter paper, therefore, he dropped the plan. (Poland, p. 409). Hill then reported that during the railroad steal fight, it was rumored that Baxter offered to sign said bill for $25,000; that he knew when the man (name never given) was in Baxter's hotel room to complete the bribery; and that he walked down past Baxter's room and heard Baxter say something like "get it fixed right, and I'll sign." (Poland Report, pp. 241-47)

Mr. Baxter, when questioned about his campaign activities, stated in essence that he had a heavy speaking schedule and never had time even to go home and vote.

As the investigation progressed, the radicals lost more ground with the committee.

The committee made its report to Congress February 6, 1875 and strongly endorsed the new government of Arkansas.[16] Poland made the main speech for adoption of the report on March 2, 1875. He denied the revolutionary phase in the adoption of a new constitution, pointing out that Baxter was no longer governor, and that it was a question then of the legality of the Constitution of 1874, stating: "It was as peaceable a change as ever took place in Massachusetts, Vermont, New York, Pennsylvania, or any other state."

He admitted frauds against Brooks in the election of 1872 but said they were committed by the very men who then wanted to destroy the new constitution and install Brooks as governor — Clayton, Dorsey, and McClure. He spoke of the possible use of troops to destroy the new government and to reestablish the old constitution:

"The moment they [the troops] are withdrawn it [the forced government under the old constitution] will vanish like dew in the morning."

Powell Clayton, immediately after the final vote, asked his followers in Arkansas to accept the decision as final.

In 1938, George B. Rose, a member of the most outstanding legal family in Arkansas, in the annual meeting of the Arkansas Bar Association gave great credit to Federal Judge Henry C. Caldwell for encouraging Poland to stand by the new reconstructed government of Arkansas. Caldwell, an officer in the Federal Army, had been appointed by Lincoln as judge of the Eastern District of Arkansas to replace Judge John Ringo, who supported the Confederacy. Rose said Caldwell took Poland to his home and explained the situation in Arkansas.

About 1890 Judge Caldwell was appointed to the U.S. Circuit Court of Appeals in Los Angeles by President Harrison. After retiring, he considered Arkansas his real home and returned to Little Rock often to visit his daughter. He died February 15, 1915.

The oppression of the Clayton-Hadley years left Arkansas financially stripped and heavily indebted. Recovery from this condition proceeded slowly for over 20 years. Prices declined in nearly all industrial and farm products and wages, continuing through the gold-silver contest of the nineties and recovering only in the next century.

This struggle was a part of the dying embers of the Civil War. From May 11 to 16, 1911, one of the last Confederate Veteran Reunions was held in Little Rock and Hot Springs. So many came — over 100,000 — that neither city could hold them all. President Taft sent them a message of unity which will be long remembered:

> The men of the Confederate Army fought for a principle which they believed to be right and for which they were willing to sacrifice their lives, their homes — in fact all these things which men hold most dear. As we recognize their heroic services, so they and their descendants must honor the service rendered by the gallant sons of the North in the struggle for the preservation of the Union. The contending forces of nearly a half century ago have given place to a united North and South and to an enduring union.

Since the Civil War, Arkansas has met and conquered innumerable challenges and has become a leader in many areas of American life. Fortunately, the people of the state have been able to take the trials of the past and use them as valuable lessons for the future.

FOOTNOTES

[1] *Arkansas Gazette*, May 24, 1974, 1-3.
[2] *Ibid.*, May 24, 1874, 1-3.
[3] *Ibid.*, July 7, 1874, 2-3.
[4] *Ibid.*, July 15, 1874, 1-1.
[5] *Ibid.*, July 24, 1874.
[6] *Ibid.*, September 11, 1874, 1-4.
[7] *Ibid.*, September 10, 1874, 1-3.
[8] *Ibid.*, September 10, 1874, 1-8.
[9] *Ibid.*, September 11, 1874, 1-4.
[10] Letter to author from Mrs. Helen Lindley, Editor, *The Izard County Historian*, May 5, 1980.
[11] Letter from Helen Lindley, Editor, *The Izard County Historian*, Dolph, Arkansas and letter from Dr. Billingsley.
[12] *Arkansas Gazette*, June 11, 1874, 1-4.
[13] *Ibid.*, September 11, 1874, 1-1.
[14] Fayetteville *Democrat*, November 14, 1874.
[15] *Arkansas Gazette*, February 17, 1874, 1-1.
[16] Arkadelphia *Southern Standard*, March 6, 1875, 2-4.

Chapter 15

What Became of the Radicals?

People ask, "What became of the radicals?" Many went back home (no one knows how many), but more went west, for their reputations were too poor to take home. Most of the West was then divided into territories. President Grant gave them appointments from governor to postal employee.

Catterson, Upham, Sarber, and several others were made deputies in the two federal courts of Arkansas, but we find little mention of them later. Upham may have feared reprisal, for he moved to Oxford, Mississippi, and died about ten years later.

C.B. Fitzpatrick went to Texas, and the press soon reported that he was killed. W.J. Hynes ran for city attorney in Chicago but was defeated.

Judge William Story, after resigning to prevent impeachment,[1] went to Ouray, Colorado, carved out a fairly successful career in law, banking, and mining, and was elected lieutenant governor of Colorado in 1892, serving one term.[2] His short biography, which perhaps he wrote, gave ill health as his reason for leaving the federal judgeship of the Western District of Arkansas,[3] when it was actually to prevent impeachment.

Joseph Brooks

Joseph Brooks, after his defeat, apparently made two unsuccessful trips to Washington to get President Grant to overturn the 1874 Constitution and restore the government to the radicals. He remained very active and ambitious in radical politics in Arkansas for a couple of years and he offered to be a candidate. He never again associated with the conservative wing of the Republican Party.

President Grant appointed Brooks postmaster of Little Rock March 19, 1875.[4] He became ill in 1877 and died April 25.[5] The press gave no cause of his early death at 57, but surely the stress of his unsuccessful and turbulent political career contributed to it. His background at Northwestern University and in the ministry indicated potential for a more fruitful life than he led. The only achievement of Brooks in the coup and during Baxter's term as governor was to destroy himself as a conservative. His surrender to Powell Clayton was a major mistake which in his last quiet days he might have regretted. He is buried in the Methodist Belfontain Cemetery in St. Louis. His daughter, Ida Jo Brooks, remained in Little Rock as a practicing physician.

Powell Clayton

Powell Clayton moved his official residence from Little Rock, where he was never well accepted, to Eureka Springs. There he and his friends built the grand Crescent Hotel, his home, and promoted the Missouri and North Arkansas Railroad running eventually from Seligman, Missouri, to Helena, Arkansas.

Clayton never again received more than three or four votes in the legislature for the U.S. Senate and was succeeded by Augustus Garland in 1877. He was chairman of the Arkansas Republican Party until the administration of the Democratic President, Woodrow Wilson. He helped dispense patronage and was appointed ambassador to Mexico by President McKinley in 1897.

Had Clayton tried seriously to make a comeback in Arkansas politics he would have met Republican opposition as well as Democratic. Clayton, however, spoke for the Republican Party in the national campaigns in the North.

The *Arkansas Gazette* reprinted a short item from the Pittsburg *Leader*, a Republican paper:

> While Judge Kelly's speech of last night was interesting, powerful, and thorough, that of Powell Clayton, who followed him, while it may have been interesting to those fond of vulgar witticisms, was light and most indecent.

The article said that Lynch, a black man from Mississippi, should replace Clayton as a speaker.[6]

About a month before Clayton died, his book *Aftermath of the Civil War in Arkansas* was published. It was a tangle of praise for everything the radicals did and a condemnation of everything that the people of Arkansas did, stating that Baxter's recovery of the governorship in 1874 was the most disgraceful occurrence in Arkansas history. The criminal acts of the radicals were not mentioned. Clayton died August 25, 1914, and was buried in Arlington, Virginia.

John M. Clayton

John M. Clayton returned to Pine Bluff after the radical stranglehold on Arkansas was broken in 1874. The black vote there was strong and supported Clayton, and he served five terms as sheriff. Rather than have a bloody fight over every election, the two parties, perhaps wisely, divided the several positions between them.[7] The office of sheriff, being a fee position and one where script could be bought cheap and turned in for cash, probably made considerable money for Clayton.

The Republicans won the national Congressional race in 1888, and Clayton then ran for U.S. Representative against Clifton Breckinridge, nephew of John C. Breckinridge, Democratic candidate for President in 1860. Breckinridge won, 17,857 to 17,011. If Clayton could have proven fraud, the House probably would have seated him rather than Breckinridge. Thus, he traveled over the district seeking the evidence of fraud. On election day at Plumerville (near where serious militia encounters occurred in 1868) a sharp quarrel had gone on between the two parties involving the election of officers, and the ballot box was stolen. Clayton probably would have carried that precinct but not by enough and took affidavits from people who said they voted for him. As he sat in his abode in the early night January 29, 1889, he was shot to death. The killers were not identified. Since Clayton's wife had died five years earlier, this crime left six orphan children.

John McClure

John McClure had little opportunity to advance in Arkansas, even though he tried. He ran for U.S. Representative against a badly divided Democratic opposition and came close to being elected. He had ambitions of becoming a federal judge when Judge Caldwell was appointed to the Circuit Court of Appeal, but another got the position. Ironically, he advised the Republican Party to get rid of the blacks, claiming that a white Republican Party would grow. The Democrats then for 30 years chided the Republicans about this fight as the lily whites versus the black and tan.

McClure died in Little Rock July 7, 1916.

W. W. Wilshire

W.W. Wilshire was part of the Powell Clayton wing of the radical Republican Party until he saw the good that Elisha Baxter was doing for the state and then became a Baxter supporter. He was appointed Chief Justice of the Arkansas Supreme Court in 1868, the first under the Reconstruction regime but resigned while the court had the James M. Johnson quo warranto case under consideration in 1872. This case was deliberately hatched against Johnson by the

Clayton ring. Whether he resigned in disgust over the court's behavior, because of pressure from Clayton to decide matters as the ring desired, or to run for U.S. Representative, has never been explained but perhaps it was all three.[8]

In 1872 Wilshire ran for U.S. Representative as a Republican against Thomas M. Gunter of Fayetteville, who ran on the combined ticket of the Democrats and the revolting Greeley Republicans. That latter group was strongest in northwest Arkansas because it was the home of most of the Unionists. The Unionists supported Gunter as did most of the Democrats. This election was close, but the certificate was given to Wilshire. Congress (thoroughly radical Republican) seated him temporarily by a very small majority. There was a Gunther in Sebastian County politics, and many wrote in the name "Gunther," and others misspelled his name.[9]

Soon after Elisha Baxter took office, Wilshire began speaking in Congress and writing to Arkansas in support of Baxter. He first did this when the railroad bond steal bill came up. But when the real battle began in 1874, Wilshire was the only Congressman who aided Baxter. The other four, two senators and Representatives M.L. Bell and Asa Hodges, and the Democratic contender, Gunter, supported Brooks.

As a result of Wilshire's stand, the radical House of Representatives immediately found that Gunter, though a Democrat, had been elected instead of Wilshire. Wilshire then came back to Arkansas a hero, reaching Little Rock May 28. A huge crowd, in appreciation of the stand that this carpetbagger had made for Baxter, met the train. They made a procession three blocks long as they marched to the Anthony House.

The General Assembly invited him to address the joint session, and he gave credit to Attorney General George H. Williams in the recent troubles and suggested that Baxter's ample guards in May 1873 brought him his favorable *quo warranto* decision.[10]

Candidates for U.S. Representatives were then nominated by district conventions. The Democratic congressional convention of the third district met at Clarksville September 25, 1874, and nominated Wilshire against two outstanding Southern men, Jordan Cravens and Jabez M. Smith. Wilshire went back to the House as a Democrat.[11]

Since Wilshire had been first associated with the Republican Party and the radicals, the *Arkansas Gazette*, realizing that he needed help to overcome his former associations, gave him more than usual support, telling the Democrats and conservatives of the work he did for the conservatives in the Brooks revolution, and he was elected.

In Congress he worked to get a donation of federal land for the State University and public schools. After one term in the House, Wilshire retired voluntarily to the practice of law in Washington, D.C., Even while in Washington, he took some part in Arkansas affairs. In 1880 he, along with Augustus H. Garland, opposed the Fishback effort to secure the repudiation by Arkansas of the Holford bond debt and of the railroad and levee bond debt created during the radical period. They were successful that year, but Fishback was persistent, and he succeeded in getting repudiation adopted in the general election of 1884.

Wilshire was not in good health, and he died August 19, 1888, in Washington. His body was returned to Little Rock for burial in the Mount Holly Cemetery.

William Henry Harrison Clayton

This Clayton was a brother of Powell, and a twin of John M. Clayton. He served in the Federal Army and was in the campaigns of Antietam and Chancellorsville. Though a recipient of several appointments during the regime of his older brother, he was never directly associated with any of the scandals of that time.

Immediately after the radicals lost control of Arkansas, Clayton resigned as judge of the Fifth Judicial District, and Grant appointed him federal district attorney to the court of the Western District of Arkansas in Fort Smith along with the famous Judge Isaac Parker.[12] He served in that position until the Democrat Grover Cleveland was President. President Harrison reappointed him in 1889.[13]

Apparently the success of Judge Parker's court in hanging about 88 criminals was greatly due to Clayton's vigorous prosecutions, for he convicted more than 75 of first-degree murder, and over half of them paid the penalty on the scaffold in the historic jail yard at Fort Smith.[14]

It was the prosecution on March 7, 1881, of a group of whites, known as "Boomers," who illegally invaded the Cherokee Nation in what is now Oklahoma, then led by Chief Bushyhead, which gave Clayton good standing with the Indians.

Due to the good relationship established with the Indians in that case, Clayton in 1897 was appointed federal judge for the newly formed court in Indian Territory with headquarters at McAlester. Congress in 1906 passed a bill to combine Indian Territory, Oklahoma Territory, and Cherokee Nation into the State of Oklahoma. Clayton was given considerable supervisory control over the districting of Indian Territory for delegates to the constitutional convention and the certification of the delegate election.[15] He was fair in advising the Indians to elect delegates to represent them.

This court ended when Oklahoma became a state in 1907, and Judge Clayton formed a law partnership in McAlester with his son, W.H.H. Clayton, Jr., as Clayton and Clayton.

Judge Clayton's behavior was not radical, unlike most of the other resettled northerners who followed politics.

Thomas M. Bowen

Of all the radicals who left Arkansas that fateful year of 1874, Thomas M. Bowen perhaps achieved the greatest career with the greatest acclaim from the people where he went. The archives of Colorado show this clearly.

Immediately after the War he lived in Van Buren, married a Miss Thurston there, and associated with the conservative Jesse Turner and other well known conservative Republicans established in that section. Only after he moved his operations to Little Rock and associated with Powell Clayton after the 1868 Constitutional Convention was he classified as a radical.

In 1871, President Grant appointed Bowen Governor of Idaho, but the territory was thinly settled and plagued with Indian wars. He resigned and returned to Arkansas and ran for the U.S. Senate in 1873 only to be defeated by Stephen W. Dorsey.

After the defeat of the radicals in 1874, several of them went to the Territory of Colorado, because President Grant needed men there. A Colorado publication stated:

> In 1874 President Grant summarily displaced all Colorado officials except Moses Hallett [an excellent judge generally loved by the Colorado people]... It was a great sensation for a small western territory, which attributed the President's action to the result of a game of Poker between himself and delegate Chaffee [Jerome B. Chaffee, a Colorado political boss of giant strength there]. The Senate had not then been transformed into a board of inquisition, hence the facts were never fully disclosed, but the bar of Colorado resented the change of judges, and took pains to let its opinion be known.[16]

This quotation came from a lecture delivered April 7, 1924, at the Denver Bar Association by Charles S. Thomas at "Old Timer's Day" dinner. A more likely cause of the dismissal was that in 1874 President Grant appointed as Governor of Colorado Edward M. McCook, one of the subordinate officers of the army of the West at the Battles of Shiloh and Chickamauga. Chaffee objected to that appointment and took the fight to the U.S. Senate, which lacked only one vote in preventing the confirmation of McCook. Grant then cleaned house in Colorado. The poker game could have been just a warmup to this bigger fight.[17]

Bowen landed at Del Norte and practiced law until Colorado

became a state. He was then elected judge of the Fourth District, filled with miners and criminals. His district was a wide expanse, bigger than the state of Ohio.

This same Old Timer's lecturer mentioned above reminisced: This was Bowen's district, and Bowen was a picturesque judge. In Castilla County the Clerk was the well-known Billy Myers . . . On one occasion a jury was being empaneled in a petty criminal case during which Bowen was immersed in a newspaper of fairly recent date. When both sides announced that they would take the jury, Bowen, without looking up, said, 'Billy, swear them roosters.'

In another case, a murderer, since he pled guilty, was given a life sentence as was customary. The people disagreed, and Judge Bowen next morning found the unlucky defendant hanging out of the courthouse by his neck. Two nooses were on Bowen's desk, one for the judge and one for the prosecuting attorney. Bowen left in a hurry, never to return. Other authorities affirmed that he had little law to guide him in the many suits regarding mine claims but that he nevertheless made good decisions. Bowen became a respected judge and a millionaire in his mining operations.

Bowen's greatest case was that of the Denver & Rio Grande Railway versus the Santa Fe Railway, when both companies claimed the Royal Gorge of the Arkansas River as right-of-way, and each had a small army of men ready to fight for possession. Judge Bowen's decision favored the Denver & Rio Grande, and though it was not final, it gave that railroad such an advantage that active opposition was stopped.[18]

Although Bowen was defeated in his race for governor, he remained an ambitious man and was elected U.S. Senator in 1883. Bowen was defeated in 1889, but he served out his life on several penal commissions. He died December 30, 1906, and was long remembered as one of the more colorful men in early Colorado history.

Stephen W. Dorsey

Probably the most powerful man, excepting Powell Clayton and Thomas Bowen, to come to Arkansas and become a radical was Stephen Wallace Dorsey. His power was in national politics and in his western ventures which followed his career in Arkansas.

After losing the contest with Baxter in 1874 for the control of Arkansas, Dorsey had no more influence in the state, although he served as U.S. Senator until 1879. He tried unsuccessfully to revive the radical wing of the Republican Party which Baxter destroyed in 1874.

On January 12, 1876, Dorsey took voluntary bankruptcy in federal court in Helena, listing 37 debts totaling $183,000. He owed over $100,000 in London and Amsterdam. A fellow radical, Logan H. Root of Little Rock, was another creditor in the amount of $10,000.[19] His palatial home was auctioned and several mortgage companies fought over the proceeds.[20]

The *Gazette* teased Dorsey about his bankruptcy:
Stephen's so deceiving
The devil can't believe him.[21]

In 1880, Dorsey perhaps reached his highest point in the national Republican Party when he was secretary to the national committee. That was the year that James Garfield was elected president and Chester Arthur vice-president, and he surely expected a choice appointment.

One of the great campaigners and advisors to presidents at that time was Senator Carl Schurz, and he wrote president-elect Garfield January 2, 1881, advising him not to appoint Dorsey or several others. "Any one of them," his letter stated, "connected in any way with your administration would sink it at once in public esteem."[22]

Dorsey was soon indicted for star route mail frauds. Being high in political rank allowed him to help arrange star route mail contracts, and in May, 1881, he was tried in federal court in Portland, Oregon, for fraudulently obtaining increases in mail-carrying contracts. One of his tricks was to multiply with false petitions the number of citizens living on a route where there were only mountains and deserts. One of his letters to a worker requested that the petitions make the signatures look different. The increases he negotiated ran up to 10 to 1. His brother was a recipient of his talents.

Robert G. Ingersoll, the greatest emotional orator of America, had in 1876 at the Republican Presidential Convention nominated James G. Baline as the candidate of the party. He lost that effort but increased his fame at law and successfully defended Dorsey in this fraud. As part of his fee and to give Dorsey further needed protection, he probably became his partner and adviser.

Soon after Dorsey's Senate term ended, he was seen traveling through northeast New Mexico in a surrey pulled by four good mules. He somehow had acquired a disputed or false Mexican land grant of 600,000 acres, the *Una De Grato* (Cat's Paw). While he could not maintain this fraudulent claim, he purchased 160-acre tracts which encompassed water holes. Since the government tried not to sell a lot of land to one man, he purchased many claims in the name of his employees or in fictitious names. This gave him practical control of approximately one million acres.[23]

He chose a site for a home about 20 miles east of the present town of Maxwell and built a flamboyant house of red sandstone which eventually became a social center of that part of New Mexico. He had large fountains, extensive gardens, and his wife's name, "Helen," spelled in flowers.[24]

Dorsey eventually sold cattle in lots of 10-25,000 but his biggest sales were the stock in his various cattle companies organized each year. He established offices in New York and in London, but his European stock-buying customers learned to look with considerable suspicion upon his stock sales. His American buyers were not so flush with money and knew him better,[25] and the European buyers soon found him out.

Others in partnership with him were Ozra A. Hadley, who followed him from Arkansas, and Adelaide Danforth, Hadley's daughter, who married Keyes Danforth. Keyes had been Governor Clayton's private secretary and Hadley's private secretary while the latter was acting governor of Arkansas prior to the term of Elisha Baxter, but Keyes Danforth is not mentioned in the New Mexico venture.[26]

Dorsey remained a prominent Republican and a part of the Santa Fe political ring. He took part in cattlemen's associations, the Grand Army of the Republic, and prominent social sets of New Mexico. He remained a friend and admirer of Powell Clayton and named his son Clayton.

After about ten years in cattle ranching, Dorsey transferred to an irrigation project, Henry Irrigation Company, in central Colorado. Some people felt that he left New Mexico broke, but since he kept many investments in the name of his wife, Helen, others felt that he always had plenty. For many years his story in cattle raising was told and retold in New Mexico. A search of the Colorado archives fail to show any reference to the Henry Irrigation Company.

Dorsey's mansion, though now deteriorated, still stands in New Mexico, and has been purchased by the state for restoration as an example of the 19th century architecture.[27]

While Dorsey was U.S. Senator, a county in Arkansas was carved out of Jefferson, Lincoln, Grant, and Bradley, and it was named Dorsey County. Other union and radical names attached to counties were Lincoln, Clayton, Grant, and Sarber. When the radicals lost power in 1874, Clayton County became Clay, and Sarber became Logan. Grant and Lincoln Counties remained. When Cleveland became the first post-Civil War Democratic president, Dorsey County was renamed Cleveland County, and a few Arkansans today know that we once had a U.S. Senator named Dorsey who had a county named for him.

Dorsey's military service, beginning at 19 years of age, was fairly long. He volunteered for the Ohio Light Artillery on August 23, 1861, and was discharged at Cleveland June 15, 1865. He was in many major battles in both the western and eastern fronts, receiving a number of promotions, the last as major for gallant service at Wilderness, Spottsvania, Cold Harbor, and Petersburg. He affirmed in his pension application that he was wounded three times.

In asking for a 30-day furlough in 1865, he stated that both of his parents had recently died and that their estate was being looted at home. He requested the furlough to take care of his family affairs. After the War many soldiers turned to dishonesty in business because they saw the war profits of those who stayed at home.

Dorsey died at Los Angeles March 20, 1916, and was buried in Denver where his son, Clayton Chauncey Dorsey, had practiced law with some of the city's leading politicians since 1889.

FOOTNOTES

[1] Fort Smith *Herald*, June 13, 1874, 2-6.
[2] Letter to author from Secretary of State, Colorado, July 9, 1980.
[3] *Portrait and Biographical Records of State of Colorado*, (Chapman Publishing Company, 1890), pp. 141-2.
[4] Letter to author, U.S. Postal Service, June 27, 1974.
[5] Little Rock *Evening Star*, April 30, 1877.
[6] *Arkansas Gazette*, October 23, 1884, 1-1.
[7] Pine Bluff *Commercial*, February 7, 1884, 4-5.
[8] New York *Times*, February 17, 1871, 1-4.
[9] David Walker papers, University of Arkansas Library.
[10] *Arkansas Gazette*, May 31, 1874, 1-1.
[11] *Ibid.*, September 26, 1874.
[12] Fayetteville *Democrat*, July 4, 1874.
[13] *Arkansas Gazette*, May 4, 1889, 4-1.
[14] *The Indian Journal*, Eufaula, Oklahoma, December 16, 1920.
[15] *Chronicles of Oklahoma*, Oklahoma Historical Society, 1921, Volume 48, p. 400.
[16] *The Colorado Magazine*, Vol. I. Article 6, July 1925, p. 201.
[17] *Ibid.*, Vol. 46, Article 2, p. 145, 1969.
[18] *History of Colorado*, Volume V, pp. 445-446, (Baker & Hafem, 1879).
[19] *Arkansas Gazette*, February 4, 1876, 2-4.
[20] *Ibid.*, April 28, 1876.
[21] *Ibid.*, February 9, 1876, 2-2.
[22] Putnam, Carl Schurz Speeches, Correspondence, political papers, Vol. IV, p. 83.
[23] Morris F. Taylor, "Steven W. Dorsey," *New Mexico Historical Review*, January, 1974.

[24] *Ibid.*
[25] *Ibid.*
[26] *Ibid.*
[27] *Arkansas Gazette*, July 13, 1975, 5 E-1.
[28] *Ibid.*, May 20, 1874.
[29] Pine Bluff *Commercial*, January 17, 1907, 1-1.

Bibliography

Books

Allen, James. *The Battle for Democracy* (1865-1876). New York: International Publishers, 1937.

Allsopp, Fred W. *History of the Arkansas Press.* Little Rock: Parke-Harper Publishing Company, 1922.

Barnes, Claude G. *The Tragic Era.* Boston: Houghton-Mifflin, 1957.

Bassett, John Spencer. *A Short History of the United States.* New York: The MacMillan Company, 1913.

Beard, Oliver Thomas. *A Story of War and Reconstruction.* Ridgewood, N. J.: Gregg Press, 1968.

Biographical Directory of Congress. Washington, D. C., Superintendent of Documents, U. S. Printing Office, Washington, D. C.

Burger, Nash Kerr. *South of Appomattox.* New York: Harcourt, 1959.

Franklin, John Hope. *Reconstruction After the Civil War.* Chicago: University of Chicago Press, 1961.

Clayton, Powell. *Aftermath of the Civil War.* New York: The Meade Publishing Company, 1914.

Fletcher, John Gould. *Arkansas.* Chapel Hill: University of North Carolina Press, 1947.

Globe. The Congressional Record. 1850-75.

Harrell, John M. *A History of the Reconstruction Period on Arkansas.* St. Louis: Seamson Publishing Co., 1893.

Ross, Margaret. *Arkansas Gazette: The Early Years 1819-1866.* Little Rock: Arkansas Gazette Foundation, 1969.

Staples, Thomas. *History of Reconstruction in Arkansas.* New York: Columbia University Press, 1923.

Worthen, W. B. *Early Banking in Arkansas.* Little Rock: Democratic Printing Company, 1906.

Journals

Journal of the Constitutional Convention of Arkansas, 1868.
Journal of the General Assembly of Arkansas, 1846-48.
Journal of the General Assembly of Arkansas, 1864-65.
Journal of the General Assembly of Arkansas, 1866.
Journal of the General Assembly of Arkansas, 1868.
Journal of the General Assembly of Arkansas, 1871.
Journal of the General Assembly of Arkansas, 1873.
Journal of the General Assembly of Arkansas, 1874.
Journal of the General Assembly of Arkansas, 1875.
All *Acts of Arkansas* from 1861 to 1875.

Newspapers

The Arkansas Gazette, 1840 to 1975.
The Arkansas True Democrat, 1852-1862.
The Arkansian, Fayetteville, Arkansas, 1859-1861.
The Constitutional Union, of Des Arc, Arkansas.
The Daily Republican, of Little Rock, 1867-75.
The Fayetteville Democrat, 1868-1890.
The Fort Smith New Era, 1863 to 1875.
The Helena World, 1890.
The New York Times, 1865-75.
The Southern Shield, Helena, Arkansas, 1842-1950.
The Van Buren Press, 1850 to 1875.
The Washington Telegraph, of Washington, Arkansas, 1860 to 1866.
The Southern Standard, Arkadelphia, Arkansas, 1870-80.
The Memphis Daily Appeal, 1868-80.

Unpublished Sources

Civil War and Reconstruction papers in the Arkansas History Commission at Little Rock.
Civil War and Reconstruction papers in the University of Arkansas Library, Fayetteville.
The Clara B. Eno papers in the University of Arkansas Library, Fayetteville.
Private correspondence with historical associations in Arkansas, Missouri, Pennsylvania, Georgia, Colorado, New Mexico, Texas and Louisiana, and with descendants of Elisha Baxter. Two visits to archives of Colorado and many to archives of Arkansas.

The courthouse records of Washington, Madison, Pope, Woodruff, Drew, Ashly, Chicot, Conway, Pulaski, Jefferson, Desha, and Independence Counties in Arkansas.

David Walker papers in the University of Arkansas Library, Fayetteville.

Jesse Turner papers in the University of Arkansas Library, Fayetteville.

The Kie Oldham papers in the University of Arkansas, David Mullins Library, Fayetteville.

The post-Civil War papers in the archives of the State of Colorado in Denver, to where many radicals fled.

Index

A
Advertising, 112
Amnesty, 65, 66, 95
Appointive power, 55, 138
Arkansas Gazette, 2, 3, 12, 37, 63, 71
Arkansas Industrial University, 68
Au Revoir, 99

B
Baker, Samuel, 44
Baltimore Convention (1864), 51
Bancroft, George, 14, 52
Bartlett, Liberty, 110
Baxter, Elisha, 29, 34, 83, 85, 87, 88, 91 93, 105, 112, 120, 126, 129, 137, 138, 140
Beauregard, P. T. G., 29
Berry, James H., 128, 131
Berry, James R., 120
Bishop, Albert Webb, 2
Black Codes, 4
Blair, Francis P., 24
Bland, James L., 43
Blocker, W. D., 28
Bond Refusal, 114
Bowen, Thomas, 11, 12, 63, 152
Brooks, Joseph, 14, 32, 42, 57, 71, 77, 107, 116, 117, 120, 125, 129, 147
Business conditions, 54, 66, 112
Bradley, John M., 13
Brown, B. Gratz, 76
Bull, John, 106
Bush, Uriah, 30
Butler, John, 94

C
Caldwell, Judge Henry C., 144
Catterson, R. F., 27, 38, 72, 75
Chicot County, 69, 70
Cairo & Fulton Railroad, 24
Claims (Militia), 61
Clark, George W., 33
Clayton, John M., 22, 93, 149
Clayton, Powell, 15, 17, 21, 22, 23, 28, 34, 35, 36, 42, 46, 50, 51, 52, 54, 55, 58 72, 83, 99, 106, 142, 148
Clayton, William H. H., 22, 133, 149

Constitutional Convention (1874), 138
Constitutional Eagle, 10
Constitutional Election (1868), 11
Colfax, Schuyler, 24
Controversies, 84
Conway County, 27
Curtis, General, 31

D
Danforth, Keys, 37
Danley, C. C., 2
Democratic hopefuls, 77
Dell, Valentine, 16, 82
Drew County, 45
Dorsey, S. W., 92, 114, 153
Duke, S. A., 42

E
Echo of Powell Clayton, 81
Education, 52, 53
Election (1870), 56
Edwards, General John, 24, 72
English, E. H., 105, 117
Etheridge, Y. W., 46
Extraordinary Act, 120

F
Fagan, James F., 24
Faulkner, Sandy, 28
Fayetteville Democrat, 47, 109
Fitzpatrick, C. B., 93
Fleeing Radicals, 133
Fort Smith *Tri-Weekly*, 55
Fort Smith Troops, 129
Fourteenth Amendment, 7
Frolich, Jacob, 3
Furbush, W. H., 14, 95

G
Garland, Augustus H., 28
Gibbons, John, 2, 8, 45
Gilbert, G. C., 10, 105, 110
Gill & Matthews, 46
Gillem, General, 11
Grant, U. S., 120, 123, 128
Greeley, Horace, 46, 47, 76, 86

H

Hadley, O. A., 24, 58, 63, 64
Hallie, (river boat), 125
Harrell, John M., 84
Hazeldine, William, 57
Helena World, 98
Hesper, (river boat), 32
Hindman, James C., 31
Hinds, James C., 13, 32
Hodges, Asa, 24, 93
Hodges, James L., 32
House, J. W., 59
Howard, General O. O., 9
Hunt, T. J., 124
Hunter, Rev. Andrew, 84
Hynes, William J., 84

I

Impeachment, 132

J

Johnson, Andrew, 1, 6, 8
Johnson, James M., 15, 50, 51, 54, 56, 57, 124, 141
Johnson, Robert W., 110, 122
Judex, 105
Judicial insubordination, 129

K

Ku Klux Klan, 30

L

Lady Baxter, 129
Levee Bonds, 68
Lewisburg, 45
Line of March, 109
Little, Joe, 45
Little Rock, 45, 68, 69
Losses, 129
Lovejoy, Owen, 17

M

Mallory, Sam, 55, 68
Marr, Herbert, 53
Mason, J. M., 24
Mason, Simpson, 29
McClure, John, 13, 50, 64, 65, 94, 112, 149
McDonald, Alexander, 15
McRae, Dandridge, 30
McClelland, Carter, 43
Menifee, Nimrod, 28
Metropolitan Hotel, 121
Military Districts, 8
Militia, 35, 36
Militia Committee, 47
Moore, N. W., 45
Monks, William, 29
Murphy, Isaac, 1, 2, 6, 7, 9, 17, 89

N

Nettie Jones, (tug boat), 32
Newton, R. C., 88, 111, 133
New York Times, 3, 7, 15, 45, 60, 99, 105, 118, 127
New York Tribune, 45

O

Ord, General Edward O. C., 9

P

Padgett, W. R., 57
Page, Henry, 9
Parker, J. H., 30
Peek, Thomas C., 64
Penitentiary threat, (Joseph Brooks), 77
Phillips, Wendell, 3, 76
Pierce, George S., 10
Pike, Albert, 122
Pindall, X. J., 97
Platform, 1872, 92
Poland, Luke, 143, 144
Price, John G., 49
Prigmore, Captain, 42, 43

R

Radicals, 8, 114
Ray, J. C., 38
Registration, 11, 25
Republican, 10, 14, 100
Rice, B. F., 15
Railroad Bonds, 67
Railroad Steal Bill, 96
Reynolds, General John J., 4
Rogers, Anthony, 52
Root, Logan H., 72
Rose, U. M., 28, 29, 123
Royston, Grandison D., 138

S

St. John's Academy, 105, 113
Saline County, 85
Sarber, J. N., 24
Schofield, General J. M., 32
School Bill (first), 6
Schurz, Carl, 71
Scrip, 54
Shall, David F., 122
Shame, (1873 legislature), 95
Shelton, Blackwell, 14
Sherman, William T., 72
Smith, General C. H., 9, 49
Smith, V. V., 113, 128
Snyder, Oliver P., 24
Stanton, Edward M., 6
Stephens, Thaddeus, 5
Stephenson, Mattie, 18
Stephenson, M. L., 115

Story, William, 60, 113
Sumner, Charles, 5, 113

T

Taft, William H., 144
Tankersley, Charles, 56, 64, 92
Tax rate, 100
Tobias, John N., 16
Tourtellotte, Captain J. E., 39
Turner, Benton, 96

U

Unionist, 4
Upham, D. P., 24, 37, 43, 44, 45

V

Vance, Enoch, 88

W

Waste Howling Wilderness, 41, 78
Welles, Gideon, 11, 32
Western District Court, 60
Wheeler, Stephen, 35
Whence Radicals, 147, 156
White, H. King, 121, 122, 125, 138, 140, 141
White, J. T., 14, 97
White, R. B., 14
Whipple, W. G., 72
White River Journal, 111
Whytock, Judge John, 117
Williams, George H., 119, 127
Wilshire, W. W., 98, 120, 129, 142
Woodruff County, 44